Room to Grow

Transition to the Kingdom

NORM GAGNON

Originally Copyright © 2015 Norman Gagnon, Laura Gagnon. Revised May 2023.

Xpect A Miracle Ministries
ISBN: 10:1522815821
ISBN: 978-1522815822

CONTENTS

INTRODUCTION

"You transplanted a vine out of Egypt; You drove out the nations and planted it.
You cleared the ground for it, and it took root and filled the land." Psalm 80:8,9

Have you ever said to yourself, "There must be more to my Christian walk than what I am experiencing?" I was the pastor of a small church in Southern California for many years and the cry of my heart was for more of God. Little did I know what would be involved as God answered that prayer. Time and time again, I am reminded how little we know of God's ways. The methods that He uses to answer our prayers are always unexpected!

I was raised in a Christian family and was the son of a pastor. My father pastored a Pentecostal church in Montreal, Quebec for many years before he passed away. I was familiar with the Bible stories as well as the church history of great men doing great things for God. I personally witnessed miracles and many answers to prayer through my father's ministry as well as my own. Despite these things, I still felt a lack of faith and vision. The things I had experienced seemed very small and insignificant compared to the New Testament example of the church represented in the Bible. I knew God does not fail, so I had to start looking within for all the reasons why my life, my faith and my ministry were bound. I questioned everything and evaluated the call of God in my life. I wondered why I didn't sense more of an anointing in my life and ministry. The more questions I asked, the more dissatisfied I became, but I felt weakened to do anything about it. As I searched for answers, it became a very deep burden on my heart. I began to truly understand the heart wrenching cry of David as he wrote in Psalm 118:5, "In my anguish I cried to the Lord and He answered me by setting me free."

God did indeed set me free. It was a necessary but very painful process that involved a marriage failure, divorce and failure in ministry. It is amazing how we yearn for freedom in Christ and by the power of what He has done, we have the opportunity for the yokes of this world to be broken off of us, and then the Lord places His yoke on us. Lamentations 3:27-28 says, "It is good for a man to bear the yoke while he is young. Let him sit in silence for the Lord has laid it on him." The discipline of the Lord is a good thing because although it may chafe at times, it also teaches us valuable lessons. At my baby dedication on January 10, 1958 it was prophesied that God was raising me up among my family to be a Joseph for my generation. I had three older brothers and, like Joseph, they all felt I was spoiled by my parents. Thankfully, they did not try to sell me into slavery. Although, at the age of seventeen, I dedicated my life to Christ and to follow the Lord, I would soon discover that the next 25 years were going to be as close to being in prison as I could relate to. I answered the call of God and moved to Southern California to attend Bible College. At the end of the Jesus Revolution in Southern California, the Holy Spirit was still doing incredible things, especially among the younger generation. Calvary Chapel experienced a growth explosion and there was a great need for ministerial training. The Bible college I attended in San Diego opened in 1971, and it was the divine timing of the Lord as it provided much needed ministerial training for hundreds of young people during the Jesus Movement. This was my first yoke in disciplining my life to study and read the word of God. I was always embarrassed when others excelled in reading assignments because I fought to learn and stay focused. It was difficult to maintain my attention on the pages of a book. Today, this would be diagnosed as attention deficit disorder, but back then I was just criticized for being a daydreamer in class. Dreaming seemed to be a big part of the problems as well as the blessings on Joseph's life, and it was on mine, too.

Joseph's dreams brought jealousy and strife in his family. My dreams and desires brought about unwise and premature decisions. As a disciple, I learned obedience through suffering with shame and embarrassment for not being the student and public speaker that I was expected to be. That yoke became a chafing for me because the motivation and discipline tools that were used to get people to study harder was based on competition and the fear of humiliation. The pressure to read longer, which was difficult for someone with attention issues, always made me feel inadequate to the task. I remember needing to read my Bible in one year to qualify for the Bible Reader's Banquet, which was provided for free to those that read their Bible. Obviously, I understood the expectation to study my Bible as I was enrolled in Bible College; it was the forced competition and the fear that I wouldn't qualify for the end of the year banquet that I resented. There were many other pressures to succeed, but they were also based on competition and a fear of not being able to measure up to expectations. I always admired people who had such a love for reading and could polish off books in a short amount of time, but that wasn't me.

The shame of my failure to be that student and orator became a yoke of failure which required me to put all of my energy and strength to try to please others with my success. It caused me to lie and put on a false front. I was told that if I was to have any future in ministry I would need to be a great public speaker and orator. My frustration with trying to stay focused developed a resentment towards reading and the pressure to excel in something I found difficult. Although I did not love books or reading, as I grew older in the Lord, my appreciation for the word of God began to grow. I am grateful to the Lord for healing me of that shame and humiliation associated with the difficulty I found in learning during my younger years.

My second yoke was family. At 19, I was married to the daughter of a successful preacher and evangelist. I knew the expectations of following in his footsteps, and it was placed on me at an early age. Not only as a father, but as the husband that would provide for my family. My parents went into full time ministry later on in life. My father worked as a machinist for over 25 years before going back to Canada and pastoring full time. I was always proud and thankful for my parents. They never showed or communicated disappointment or regret towards me, even when I got into some high school issues in my teen years. I remember many times when I would fall short in school, athletics, or friendships and they were there for affirmation and appreciation. They never publicly tried to humiliate or embarrass me. My parents were always there loving me, encouraging me and they publicly shared their pride in me as their son. Their love for me was unconditional and very much appreciated. It was a harsh reality when my new in-laws did not have that same approach to me. I found there were many trials and challenges in marrying a pastor's daughter and walking into the new role as their son-in-law. I never realized the intense scrutiny I faced and the overwhelming examination of my life would be so brutal. I went from being a son that could do no wrong to a son-in-law that could do no right. I felt like it was next to impossible to please my in-laws. In their eyes, I fell so short of their expectations as to the person they wanted to groom as the heir to take over their ministry. My marriage and the ministry were both yoked to this family. It was destined for failure from the beginning, it just took 25 years for that reality to come to pass. There were many times I was shamed, emasculated and undermined in my authority as a parent, in my marriage and as a spiritual leader. I was undermined and disrespected more times than I could count. I never regretted being a father. I had always dreamed of having a family and being a father. I had a wonderful role model from my parents and wanted what they had: a family full of joy and laughter. I had not entertained the thought of divorce because I desired a family so much, but the family I inherited was nothing like what I had imagined for my life. The training for ministry and the demands placed upon me that included so much criticism, shame, and humiliation overwhelmed my marriage. Living this hypocritical, double life made it easy to justify my infidelity and disloyalty to my marriage to the point where I said, "No more. I'm done. I give up." I was tired of living under shame, condemnation and the double standard of trying to put on a false appearance. You don't have to tell a lie to live a lie. The deception is compelling when the fear of shame compels a person to fake who they are for the sake of public opinion. I became adept on what it was to conceal things and tried to hide behind the false public image vs. the reality of my private life. That wasn't my desire but I feared public humiliation more than I feared what it meant to live openly and honestly.

The financial yoke was more than I could bear for my family. It is good that we bear responsibility and stewardship over our finances, so I wanted my ministry in personal accounting to be above reproach. I came on staff when I was 26, and also did a variety of odd jobs during those early years. I had no education outside of the Bible College, only hard work and a good attitude. There was a lot of pressure to put ministry above everything else, including family. I was expected to attend all church functions, to give financially at every opportunity, and to serve whenever and wherever service was needed. These things were not optional for our family. After I graduated Bible College, it was the goal and intention of pretty much every graduate to be supported full time in ministry. It might involve raising support for missionary endeavors or traveling full time, depending upon support through honorariums, but whether you were on staff or traveling abroad you were not considered successful unless you could be supported full time. At least, this is what was communicated to me from my in-laws. The success of Christian businessmen was not in the same category as ordained clergy and made ministry their career. I realize now that standard was a form of idolatry and looking down at others simply because they were not in the category of ministry, but that was the pressure I endured and the standard to which I was held. There had always been seasonal or part-time work, and getting a full time job would have relieved some of the pressure, but the stress to provide for my family and the failure to be able to provide sufficiently led me to encourage my wife to look for full time work, and she took a job at a bank. My wife became the breadwinner of the family. This was another blow to my pride. The financial insufficiency became harder and harder to hide as one Sunday while I was preaching, my car was repossessed from the church parking lot. My resentment grew exponentially at the yoke I felt forced to wear, and the humiliation seemed like it never ended.

During this time the church sold off additional properties in an attempt to raise the funds necessary to keep things afloat. Our budget required twice the income than what we brought in. Many of the tithers and givers moved out of the high crime area where the church was located and began attending churches in better neighborhoods. The programs that once flourished under the founding pastor's leadership were no longer supported. The church felt I was inexperienced and lacked the polish of the founding pastor and would not attract new members to grow the church. A few that remained were faithful but not inclined to support the staff missionaries and programs that once flourished with the founding pastor's supporters. We closed down the K-12 school and let go of staff and teachers. There were many very upset people that were offended with our "lack of faith." They were loyal to the people who sacrificed so hard for the creation of that ministry. We relocated our Bible college to our sister church and began to disassemble the classrooms which provided student training. The renovation on the educational building was 90% complete but there was no money to complete the building project. Eventually, the church building was sold as we could not maintain the cost. My father-in-law had financial investments and wisdom for financial management that helped support the various ministries and the building projects, but when he transitioned out, his investment portfolio went with him. I started accumulating credit card debt to cover the expenses. When the church was sold, the church went through transition, but I had no vision for the upcoming year, so we met in parks and temporary facilities. Again, resentment and attacks were directed at me and I was shamed for not maintaining the founding pastor's vision for this ministry. My wife supported us financially and I had no ability to support the church and ministry founded by her father. There was a lot of guilt over that situation and the struggle with constant feelings of failure. I felt an enormous amount of shame and condemnation, which caused me to try and hide the problems with the finances, not only to try and protect the congregation from further disappointment but also to protect my ego. Gradually, I did begin to trust others with the financial issues but they were wolves in sheep's clothing, looking to manipulate the situation for their end game rather than actually helping solve the problems. I failed to get much needed answers from God. I was overwhelmed and resentful, and couldn't hear from God as to what to do because I was responding to one crisis after another. This also brought shame and embarrassment. My wife resented the church and the ministry and it took more from her and the family than it ever gave back. We did everything possible to give others the appearance that we were happy and successful, but we were miserable. It led us both into living double lives. Shame and resentment leads people into self-deception, which opens the door to sin, hypocrisy, justification of those sins, and eventually, spiritual death. People who knew me desperately tried to influence my decisions. The kids were grown and living their own lives and there seemed no point to continue to live a lie. The marriage and the ministry had been unhealthy for years, but we had gotten very good at putting on appearances. After I left, many people told me I needed to reconcile with my wife so that they (and God) could forgive me. Some may have been satisfied with that action, however I do not believe they ever would have truly forgiven me from their heart. I never would have been delivered or set free from shame and humiliation had I stayed tied to those relationships and that situation. I would have been further driven to despair, and succumbed to manipulation and control. Those things already had a choke hold on my life and my faith, and it was like being in prison. When everything fell apart, many people could not understand the choices I made, but I could not continue to live under those same conditions. I knew the hand of God was against my back, pushing me to break out of the confining circumstances. I felt as though I had been carrying a heavy weight around my neck for years, as I tried unsuccessfully to bear the frustrations of being a people pleaser. I needed to realize that I was not pleasing God. I had elevated the demands and expectations of others before Him. The fear of man does indeed bring a snare (Proverbs 29:25). The shame, failure and impossible expectations placed upon me from a young age amounted to a yoke I could not continue to wear. After many years in the ministry, all of these things contributed to my failure and resignation as senior pastor. No one wants to talk about failure because it's embarrassing, but I have since learned that the only way to overcome fear of failure is to experience it. It's terribly painful and humbling, but experience is a good teacher and it crucifies our flesh. God used the situation to take me to the cross. The good news is, once you've lost it all, God can resurrect you. He delivered me from the limitations I had placed on my faith and vision, in order to remake me into a man of the Spirit.

The last 20 years have been a journey of healing and deliverance. I have been ever so grateful for a merciful and compassionate God that restores. My heavenly father dealt with me as a beloved son. He did not punish me according to my sins and iniquities. Psalm 103:10-11 says, "He does not treat us as our sins deserve or repay us according to our iniquities. For as high as the heavens are above the earth, so great is His love for those that fear Him."

Laura and I began our walk together in the journey of deliverance and healing, and have been married for 20 years. Laura showed me a love for the word of God and it was an example of falling in love with Jesus, as He is the word. In the beginning there was the word, and the word became flesh and dwelt among us. My life came back into alignment as I learned how to connect with the love of God and spend time with Him on a daily basis. Laura is an incredible teacher of the word, a deliverance minister, and has written 10 books with many prayers for healing and deliverance. Laura was not raised in church. After many years of suffering various forms of abuse, God captured her heart and brought a deep deliverance to her life. She was set free from many demonic spirits, but it was because of what she endured that she had discernment of demons. She saw things in people and understood the motives of their hearts that were truly evil. But, because of that, those demons did everything possible to shame her and drive her away. They did not want to be uncovered or exposed. It was Satan's plan to use shame, humiliation, and failure to isolate both of us and cause bitterness towards the church. It wasn't the church's fault, but it was the spirit behind it that the enemy used to create resentment and hurt. When relationships are healthy - whether it's in the body of Christ or in a marriage, it's a real blessing. But, when it's not healthy and becomes toxic, it can cause such bitterness that people tend to want to reject all of it and throw the baby out with the bathwater. All of a sudden, the thought of going to church brings up painful memories, so people justify their disconnection from the body. The thought of marriage brings up thoughts of how bad a former experience was, and people don't know if they can trust themselves to make the commitment to someone else, and the institution of marriage comes under attack. The enemy will always help us justify disconnection and isolation, but it's important to understand that's how Satan plays his game to keep us disconnected from destiny connections. Those are covenant connections we all need in order to fulfill the plan of God for our lives. The desire is to isolate ourselves from further pain and disappointment, but it can also disconnect us from the bigger purposes God has for us. As Laura and I began this journey together, God began to give us a fresh compassion towards His bride. The Lord is so much bigger than our enemies. He will take what the enemy intended to harm us and turn it into something good. God's desire is for all of His children to be set free, healed and live productive lives so that we can help deliver others. He wants our roots to grow deep in Him and bear much good fruit. I pray that the message of transition in this book helps you navigate some of the difficulties. God has given us a beautiful promise in Isaiah 54. Do not be afraid, for you will not be put to shame. Do not fear disgrace, you will not be humiliated. God knows how to deliver us from all our fears, failures and the pain and shame of disgrace.

Transition required leaving long term relationships and moving two thousand miles away. God showed me that my faith was in external things like organizations, the covering provided by ministerial fellowships, and governing boards. I looked at diplomas and licensing as my accreditation and approval from God. I fell into the snare of believing that my security was more in the form of church rather than in my own personal relationship with the Lord.

I spent 15 years in the pastorate trying to make my mentors, congregation and family happy without success. What tremendous disappointment and discouragement I faced as I realized all my efforts were not pleasing to the one I loved so much. *Jesus.*

As I searched for answers, the portion of scripture that kept speaking to my heart was the parable of the talents found in Matthew 25. I knew the day would come when I would stand before God and He would ask me, "What have you done with the talents I gave you?" God does not call us to tolerate things that lead us into spiritual compromise. The religious spirit is deadly to the life of the church and individuals. This spirit is responsible for critical, fault finding, judgmental attitudes, and it became about maintaining the mechanics of the ministry, rather than a life-giving relationship with Jesus. My life and the state of the church was bound by many religious attitudes and the spirits that were associated with them. In Revelation 2:20 Jesus rebuked the church in Thyatira for tolerating that spirit of Jezebel because it was an ungodly spirit that brought destruction to the body of Christ. I recognized that spirit at work in my former church and knew things needed to change. I could no longer tolerate it. God wanted me to serve Him but He also required me to be uprooted from my comfort zone.

Jesus' instructions to us as found in John 15:5 was to abide in Him so that we bear much fruit. Apart from Him, we can do nothing. He used the analogy of the individual believer being likened to a branch off of the vine. If a branch of a plant is cut off from its life source, it will soon wither and die. I wanted more for my life, but it required me to come to terms with the revelation that I had been like a plant that was root bound. "Root bound" is a term used to describe a plant or vine that is constricted by its container or environment. In Matthew 13:2, Jesus gave the interpretation of the seed planted among thorns. The worries of this life, the deceitfulness of wealth, and the desires of other things came in and choked the word, making it unfruitful. The word 'choke' is translated as 'to strangle or to seize a person's throat.' When we allow the death grip of cares, worries, and distractions of life to choke the word, the very life of the Spirit can no longer breathe into that individual. The analogy of being root bound is finding yourself so entangled with the busyness of life, work, or ministry that you can no longer discern the life and breath of the vine have been choked out. The Apostle Paul stated in 2 Timothy 2:4, "No man that warreth entangleth himself with the affairs of this life, that he may please Him who has chosen him to be a soldier." (KJV)

One thing I have noticed is that when one person makes a significant change in their life and decides to leave their comfort zone (or confinements), others around them are challenged to examine their own lives. When someone you know makes life changing decisions it often reveals the fears, beliefs and insecurities of others. People sometimes struggle with that because ultimately it can end up triggering conversations, feelings, and thoughts they didn't anticipate, and may be trying to avoid. It can also reveal where people have soul wounds, offenses and judgments that are in need of healing. Others are not always comfortable with the changes that inevitably come to challenge their personal limitations in the way they think, what they believe, or the changes that will affect their own lives as a result of someone else's step outside of the "Comfort Zone." That is why true faith encounters opposition. Many people resist change due to a lack of faith or because they are unable to comprehend the bigger picture. Fear of an unknown future keeps them stuck in what's familiar, and taking steps in a new direction can seem incredibly confusing and intimidating. We often cannot see what God wants to accomplish in the midst of transition, we just have to trust Him to lead us. When a person lacks faith or foresight, they cannot discern the good that comes from change. Fear can become a powerful motivator that causes people to resist the process necessary to bring a metamorphosis and a new beginning. They can find themselves resisting what God wants to accomplish.

History is marked by people of all ages that dared to dream and take steps of faith towards an unknown future, only to meet the resistance of others. I also met with a great deal of resistance from others who were hurt, angry and fearful. My decisions affected them too, but I knew I needed to take responsibility for my failed marriage and ministry. This book is about the process God uses to transplant us from our confinements into the open field of His kingdom. His desire is to give each of us room to grow so that we become healthy and fruitful. Although it was not what I expected, I needed to have the pot of all my limitations broken so that I could be free to grow. I had been indoctrinated in a religious environment, but like the frog in the kettle analogy, I did not realize the binding of my faith was happening until my life was falling apart and I was in danger of having the life of the Spirit choked out. My roots needed to go through root shock so that I could continue to grow with the Lord. I needed to walk a deeper walk with God, and that required knowing Him in a deeper, more authentic way. It took an extended period of time to recover from everything I experienced and learn to put my trust in Him alone. I needed to recover spiritually and emotionally, and work through a long period of transition in my life that also gave me time to work through my own deliverance issues.

Transition was a very difficult process, but I have learned that God is not interested in our comfort. His goal is to bring us through the refining process as pure gold. Exposing my heart to the powerful presence of worship and inspired, prophetic preaching began the healing process. It was the preparation for the transplanting of my roots into the open field of God's kingdom. Paul warned the church in Galatians 5:1, "Stand fast therefore in the liberty wherewith Christ has set us free and be not entangled again with the yoke of bondage."

It is my desire and prayer that this book will give warning as well as encouragement. Through my experiences and God's word, I hope to encourage others to avoid the snares and traps of the 'pots' that are your comfort zone. These are the things that bind the growth of a person's faith and hinder the work of the Holy Spirit. A plant in a pot is constrained by the nature of its environment. If the plant doesn't eventually get transplanted into a more spacious place it will restrict the plant's growth and eventually shrivel and start to die. In the pages of this book, I invite you to look at the promise found in Psalms 80: 8,9. It is the Lord's desire to deliver His people from the things that restrict His dream for their lives. He wants to plant us in the kingdom so that our roots can spread out and fill the land with His grace and glory. God has a vision for every believer's life! His dream for you to achieve greatness in and through Him. He wants to set your feet in a spacious place.

Prayer to Be Healed from Shame and Humiliation

Heavenly Father,

I come before You today to ask for your healing and restoration in my life. I confess that I have been struggling with shame, feelings of rejection, disgrace and humiliation in my life. I feel weighed down by the burden of these emotions. I ask for your forgiveness for any actions or decisions, and also any words I have come into agreement with that have contributed to my feelings of shame, disgrace and humiliation.

I renounce and break all agreements made knowingly or unknowingly with the spirits of shame, humiliation, disgrace, dishonor, rejection, bitterness, fear, and insecurity, and I apply the blood of Jesus so that the enemy can no longer enforce his assignments against me. I command these spirits to be bound in the name and authority of Jesus Christ, and to leave me now, and to go to the abyss in Jesus' name.

Lord, I believe that you are a God of grace and mercy, and that you are able to deliver me and heal the deepest wounds in my heart. I ask that you would pour out your healing power upon me and that you would restore my soul. Help me to release these negative emotions I have been carrying, and to walk in the freedom that you have provided for me. Please direct me into the good plans you have for me.

I pray that you would surround me with your love and protection, and that you would give me the strength to overcome any negative emotions that come my way. I ask you to fill me with peace and joy, and that you would help me see myself as you see me: as a beloved child of God, redeemed by your grace.

Thank you, Lord, for your faithfulness and your love. I trust in your goodness and your power to heal me from shame, disgrace, humiliation and rejection. I thank you for healing me from resentment, feelings of failure and inadequacy. I ask all of these things in the name of Jesus Christ, my Lord and Savior. Amen.

CHAPTER ONE
Breaking the Pot of Limitations

"**You transplanted a vine out of Egypt**; You drove out the nations and planted it. You cleared the ground for it, and it took root and filled the land." Psalm 80:8,9

One of the greatest stories of deliverance in the Bible is found in Exodus. God brought a deliverer to a people who had grown too numerous for the land. The promise originated back with Abram when God told Abram that his descendents were to be as numerous as the stars in the sky and as the sand on the seashore. The name Abram meant 'exalted father,' but when the promise was fulfilled, God changed Abram's name to Abraham, which meant 'father of a multitude.' There are many times in scripture where God changed people's name and with it changed their identity. Changing one's name became symbolic of the journey to obtain their promise as well as their life's message. When a person has experienced failure or some other loss and is starting over, the thought of a fresh start sounds like a great idea, but there are no shortcuts with God's processes. All you can do is surrender to the process as God changes you into the man or woman He has called you to become. A new name, or a new identity, is the hope of new beginnings and blessings. Once we step out of the pot of limitations, there can be fear of the unknown, but there is also the hope of new beginnings as we begin to walk by faith, as Abraham did. Abraham learned to listen for God's voice and wait for instruction. The promise of expansion and abundance was given not only to Abraham, but to all who would inherit God's promises through faith. The fulfillment of the promise was ongoing to include future generations. The Israelites grew so much during captivity in Egypt that God's vision and promise for growth gave their Egyptian captors cause for concern. The Egyptians felt that the rapid growth of the Israelite nation would cause them to overtake their captors.

Egypt is often symbolic of sin, oppression, bondage, slavery or confinement.. It was also a land of refuge from famine for Jacob and his family. The destiny of this nation was preserved in the dream of a young man named Joseph. Although Egypt was a place of survival for God's family, it was not their final destination. God's intention is to bring people into the open field of promise. Egypt is seen as symbolic of the world; a place where we subject ourselves to the captivity of our lifestyle choices. It is also symbolic of the darkness in which we have settled, a place of compromise where we have become conditioned to the security of confinement. Unfortunately, it is also a place where our dreams fade into obscurity. You may even find yourself living there now.

1

The children of Israel became so dependent on the diet and provision of Egypt that they would have easily sacrificed the freedom of God's open field to the storehouses that were built by Joseph. They lamented by saying, "We remember the fish we ate in Egypt at no cost, also the cucumbers, melons, leeks, onions and garlic. But now we have lost our appetite because we never see anything but this manna," (Numbers 11: 5-6). Dr. Charles Simpson, in his message, "Regaining Your Spiritual Appetite," said that forgetting to be thankful is the first and foremost reason people lose their hunger for God. The Israelites grew tired of the manna and despised what God had so graciously provided. God was trying to teach them a very valuable lesson. The manna was there to teach them they were not to live only to satisfy their natural appetite, but they were to live by every word that proceeded out of the mouth of God. The bread from heaven is life to those who find them, and health to our flesh. Life is in the Word because Jesus is the Word of Life!

When we are involved in a church ministry or organization with a rich history and we are eating from the messages of a man or woman having a divine encounter with God, it becomes meat for us. We feel blessed and we rejoice at the excellent teaching that the ministry gives us at no cost. We feel fed and secure but it will become a danger to us spiritually if we depend on someone else to provide our spiritual nourishment. That spiritual hunger and thirst for more of God is the tool God uses to spur us on to seek more of Him. Losing our spiritual hunger is also to lose the very thing that will bring about the blessing of God. If we truly hunger after God and desire His blessing, it comes at a cost. We must lose something of ourselves if we are to gain Him. We must decrease and He must increase. The hungry and the thirsty are the ones that get God's attention because they are willing to pay the price.

Becoming Kingdom Conscious

Christianity has a rich history of men and women of God used in a powerful way to usher in revival. Kathryn Kuhlman, William Branham, Aimee Semple McPherson, Reinhard Bonnke and many other giants in the faith understood the dynamic life of God came alive in them and through them as they waited on the Holy Spirit. They ministered in power with deliverance, salvation and miracle healings as evidence that God validated the gospel message. Revivalists are kingdom conscious. They see the Bride and the body of Christ as a global vehicle for carrying the truth and power of God's glory to a darkened, blinded world. Religion and church orthodoxy will blind people to the spiritual impact of God's glory filling the earth. In Matthew 15:14, Jesus spoke about the religious spirit that caused spiritual blindness. Jesus said, "Leave them; they are blind guides. If the blind lead the blind, they will both fall into a ditch." He taught on the fact that blindness comes from elevating the traditions of men and teaching them as though they were the words from God himself, but they overlooked the defilement in their own hearts. They couldn't see the King of Kings for who He was because they compared themselves to others, evaluated themselves by their own standard, and elevated their rules and critical judgments above the word of God. In other words, they replaced revelation and a pursuit of His presence with their own thoughts and opinions, and made a god of their own understanding. The religious crowd were the blind leading others into blindness. They could not see people with compassion because they focused on the rules and laws of their traditions. The religious acted as spiritual gatekeepers that categorized people into groups of clean vs. unclean. A religious spirit keeps score and a record of wrongs. They

2

missed the mark because they didn't understand the heart of God that wanted authentic connection with those who were broken, so that people could experience grace, love, healing and forgiveness of sins. The Pharisees were said to be blind leaders because they were under the influence of a wrong spirit that blinded them to understanding and experiencing the love of God, His tender compassion and mercy. They emphasized keeping the rules and traditions of their forefathers, but couldn't recognize the Son of God when He was right there in their midst. Legalism negated the grace of God through the influence of deceptive and false teaching. While it can sound Biblical, the spirit behind it is intended to yoke people to the enemy through fear, intimidation and control instead of allowing them to walk out their relationship with God in truth, grace and liberty. They were so oblivious to their own poor spiritual condition they failed to realize they needed to repent. Jesus was not about keeping up appearances but about the condition of people's hearts. He did not completely abandon the practices of Israel, but He came to show them a better way to understand the heart of their laws.

Galatians 5:4 tells us that if we try to work to obtain our righteousness, we have fallen away from grace. The religious spirit tells you that you don't deserve grace and you haven't done enough to prove that you've repented, so you constantly feel overshadowed by guilt and condemnation. These feelings make you try to earn acceptance from others. Forgiveness becomes conditional upon your performance to satisfy the demands of others, and it feels like you are never quite 'good enough.' I found that there were many things in my own belief system that needed a major overhaul as God brought deliverance from unhealthy, unbelieving mindsets. It is comforting to know that at any time, when we truly want to be made whole, we can call on the name of Jesus and be translated out of blindness and into redemption.

Taking the Constraints off Holy Spirit

God has changed my heart to the cry of a revivalist. Revivalists are not birthed into religion. They are birthed outside of the religious system for many reasons. First, it brings the gospel message back to a state of purity and power. The true gospel demands repentance in order to purify our hearts so that the message we speak is not tainted with mixture. It is time to repent for relegating the Holy Spirit to some back room where He is not allowed to minister to His people. It is time to repent for the way we have put constraints upon the church and blocked the flow of the Spirit. The agendas of men have taken a priority above the ministry of the Holy Spirit in many, many churches and it has dishonored Him. For many years, the focus seems to have been on church growth when it should have been on influencing the culture with the Kingdom of God, for there can be no real kingdom influence without an infusion of the Holy Spirit. He is the master builder. The Holy Spirit imprint has always been about touching the body in the supernatural to advance the Kingdom of God. We must acknowledge that we are powerless and lost without His leading, and declare that we are dependent upon the Holy Spirit to advance the Kingdom of God. The pursuit of His presence must take priority above all other interests.

The Importance of Worship-Intercession

Second, revivalists want a different structure that is not entangled with confinements. They know the importance of waiting on God for the right message to the right crowd, at the right time. In order for a revivalist to make an impact, they speak about the presence of the Holy Spirit and demonstrate the power of the Kingdom of God. Worship-intercession must come first. This is a combination of worship, listening to what the Holy Spirit is speaking, and following it up by praying into it. It is to make powerful Spirit led decrees in partnership with God to act upon those declarations. We offer praise and thanksgiving for what God is doing to release breakthroughs. This sort of intercession also prays to break strongholds and invite the power of God to wage war against the powers of darkness so that others may be set free. Another way of inviting the Holy Spirit to move is through the message of the kingdom that brings repentance and deliverance.

Unity of the Spirit

The third manner in which the Holy Spirit breathes upon His people is through unity in the Spirit. We need a move of the Holy Spirit to unify the body of Christ. Our love for Jesus and His holy presence moves us to unify our language of love to cross barriers and walls of division. We must see the church (the body of Christ) as the vehicle to advance the kingdom. We cannot afford to see individual little kingdoms scattered throughout our cities. In any given city there is one collective church that belongs to the Lord Jesus Christ. Pastors must work together to form healthy relationships with other ministry leaders, as well as their own congregation members to ensure the health of the body and preserve unity. We cannot afford to have the mindset that tells us it is not a high priority to make the effort to know one another, because fostering relationships builds trust. May the Lord forgive us for seeing others as competitors and comparing our ministries with others. This can invite jealousy and competition. The accuser whispers into our ears to *divide,* and he often does that through suspicion, jealousy and comparison. The accuser always wants to suggest reasons we should distrust others, and he will often remind us of all the reasons why it's safer to keep to ourselves and our own little circle. The illusion that it is somehow safer is deceptive, because pastors and ministers have been hurt and betrayed far too often by those in their inner circle. Strength is multiplied in the presence of believers that come together in love, friendship and prayer support for one another. It builds up the hedge of protection around the city and acts as a shield of defense against the attacks of the enemy. But, the real blessing comes as unity releases the power of multiplication. It causes the anointing to flow in greater strength. Psalm 133 says, "How good and pleasant it is when God's people dwell together in unity! It is like precious oil poured on the head, running down on the beard, running down Aaron's beard, down the collar of his robe. It is as if the dew of Hermon were falling on Mount Zion. For there the Lord bestows His blessing, even life forevermore." In ancient Israel, people shared responsibilities in small communities. There was a blessing that soothed (oil), and (dew) refreshed the people that dwelled together in unity. People celebrated each other's victories and accomplishments. There was joy in the simple pleasure of sharing each other's lives and sharing meals together. That is where relationships were strengthened. As a result, the anointing increased and began to flow to touch others. This is what honors the Holy Spirit.

Forming One Spiritual Language

4

ROOM TO GROW

The fourth thing in paving the way for revival is to come back to unity of the Spirit by forming one spiritual language. The language of the Spirit is found by sharing dreams, visions, prophetic revelation and spiritual insights with one another. In Acts 2:17, God promised to pour His Spirit out on all people. Our sons and daughters will prophesy, young men will see visions, and old men will dream [divinely prompted] dreams again. We all have a piece of the revelation, but it's when we get together and share what God is saying with others that we can have a more complete, accurate picture of what God is communicating. We can then partner with Him as builders under the authority of the Holy Spirit to rebuild the ancient cities and restore the waste places.

Many great men and women of God have left powerful legacies for us to learn from. They are never to be forgotten, but they are not our destination. I personally experienced the latter rain teaching that started in a Bible College in Canada, which came as part of a movement in 1948. It was a tremendous outpouring of worship and the revelation of the doctrine known as laying on of hands. Those who experienced that movement had strong convictions towards that doctrine. They had the desire to pass on that conviction to other generations. We were taught that God burned a message into a man, and that message, when God breathed on it, became a movement. Due to man's desire to maintain those experiences, he tends to build machinery to keep the movement going. When that happens, the anointing from that movement is lost and what's left is a monument to the past. I received tremendous teaching from this movement. However, if I had kept looking back to the history of 1948, it would have kept me from looking forward and anticipating the new things God wanted to accomplish. It can be very easy to miss the new move of God when we're constantly referring to what He did in the past. The tendency is to think that He will move in a similar fashion rather than to seek Him for something completely new and different. It can become constricting when the experiences of those who were touched by a previous generation constrain the next generation in finding the next move of God. These men and women were signposts in history along the highway to God's ultimate plan.

We must be careful not to set up monuments to the past and lose sight of what God wants to do in the present or in the future. It is wonderful to honor those who have gone before us, but let us be mindful not to get stuck in the past, or even try to keep something alive that has run its course. We need to be able to discern when something is from yesterday's move of God, or simply a former season where we accomplished all we were there to do. There are seasons and times when God has something new for us, and He may want us to pass the baton to someone else. If we no longer have the grace or desire to keep doing what we've been doing, or if God seems to have lifted His hand from the work, it's time to ask Him if He wants you to prepare for something else. If you find that none of your efforts are producing and you sense God wanting to prune some things from your life that are not bearing fruit, it's time to ask Him for His plan. Sometimes we realize that the thing that seemed like it was God in a former season was actually a counterfeit to the real thing. Be willing to let go of what is not producing. He will ask us to lay down things that detract from our fruitfulness. He will separate us from certain relationships in order to bring us new ones so that we continue to bear much fruit. God tests us so that we can discern any wrong motives, misplaced trust issues, idolatry and things we are attached to that result in divided loyalties. He waits for us to surrender our fears, insecurities, and disappointment and come to a place of surrender. Until we come to a place of surrender and humility, we really can't hear clearly. When finances dry up and the doors of provision keep closing, those can be signs that God wants to do something different and align us elsewhere. Transition involves letting go of the old and taking steps to be ready to receive the new thing. Sadly though, many people have built their own kingdom and have put so much effort into it, they cannot bear to lay it all down. That is when you know you've made that good work an idol, because none of this belongs to us. If we are truly planted in the kingdom, we must acknowledge that everything belongs to the Lord. The scripture in Isaiah 43:18-19 says, "Forget the former things, do not dwell on the past. See, I am doing a new thing! Now it springs up. Do you not perceive it? I am making a way in the wilderness and streams in the wasteland." We serve a God that is always looking forward and we must learn to discern the times. That is not to say that God is so progressive that He is willing to compromise on issues such as the definition of sin and other moral absolutes found in scripture. There are many ministries today that have gone through spiritual decline. What began in the Spirit and had powerful results has, in many cases, taken on the spirit of the flesh. Man's self-effort and the desire to hold onto the reputation or the impact of yesterday's glory does not honor God. We need not struggle to hold onto something that has run its course; to do so would mean forfeiting the anointing and the power of God.

I faced a personal challenge in this area as I considered all my obligations and commitments. The pastor who I served under was given a vision for opening a Bible college to train young men and women in the teachings of the 1948 movement. When I assumed the ministry from this pastor who retired, the obligation became a restraint and my own personal container. I tried unsuccessfully to keep the Bible college open and his vision alive. Although I believed in the teachings and the need to train men and women in Bible truths, I had no personal vision burning in my heart in regards to this ministry. I was planted in a church, but I wasn't planted in the kingdom. I was given the church to continue his vision without personally hearing from God as to what He wanted me to do. One of the biggest temptations a person can face is to walk into an opportunity for which they have not paid the price. There is a process God takes each person through to prepare them for promotion. Pastors or ministers going through transition must relinquish their ministry to a man or woman who is planted in the Kingdom of God and hearing from God for themselves. That may sound like common sense, but it's not always the easiest to discern. It can be very overwhelming when the many voices of reason, other people's expectations and agendas, as well as our own thoughts come to drown out the still, small voice of God. Sometimes we want so much for something to be God we can end up convincing ourselves that what we want is God's will, when the reality may be much different. One of the worst things about transition is that we can allow impatience to get the better of us, and we begin to make an Ishmael for ourselves. I know many people in ministry face some of the same challenges. We must be honest with ourselves and with God, and ask ourselves if we are more intent on building our own kingdom and our own reputation, or His.

There are many good people with good intentions, pastors included, that cannot tell the difference between building God's kingdom or building their own. There comes a time in every person's life, if they are truly following Christ, where God will ask them to lay their Isaac on the altar and surrender it to Him. There will be trials by fire. There will be trials and testing to see whether what we have built is wood, stubble, or hay, or if they have eternal value in the kingdom. If you find yourself holding onto something and it's no longer where God is moving in a powerful way, place it in God's hands and let Him exchange it for something of eternal value. One of the misconceptions we have is the thought that we have to continue doing what we've been doing, when that season may have ended. It's a natural assumption, but I have known many people, myself included, that were under a wrong assumption. Sometimes

God calls us to lay the groundwork for a ministry and then once it's up and functioning, He asks us to pass the baton to someone else. We struggle with that thought, because we have done the hard work of breaking new ground, and sometimes it can feel very disappointing to leave our hard work in the hands of someone else. Let God bring about something with a fresh anointing, power and impact. In this day and in this hour, God is changing wineskins and the former model for doing church. He will not put the new wine into an old wineskin!

The Challenges of Transition

Transition in a person's life can be a challenging and transformative process. As we move from one stage of life to another, we often experience a range of emotions and challenges. One way to understand this process is by comparing it to the process of transplanting a plant. Both require careful planning, preparation, and attention to detail in order to ensure a successful outcome. The comfort we have during a time of transition is the fact that even though things seem chaotic and uncertain to us, God knows exactly what he's doing. There is comfort in God's promises. Psalm 37:23-24 says, "The steps of a man are ordered by the Lord who takes delight in his journey. Though he falls, he will not be overwhelmed, because the Lord is holding his hand."

We cannot receive the newness of what God has for us without a sacrifice and a divine exchange. Laying down the things that have our heart is a sacrifice that pleases the Lord. He knows what He has in mind to bring greater fruitfulness and what is called for in this hour. Those that want to keep in step with Jesus must keep their eyes on Him and follow Him wherever He goes. It is not the other way around! Jesus does not *follow us* in our own self-will wherever *we* go. If we choose not to follow Him, we will get left behind and we will sacrifice the anointing along with it. Many people tend to forget that God has a bigger dream than what we can imagine, and a definite God-sized plan to put the pieces in place to establish that dream in reality. His destiny is a land flowing with abundance in an open field. God has a bigger dream than what we can imagine. His destiny is a kingdom without borders.

Breaking Free From Our Comfort Zone

Let us think about the analogy of the potted plant. It is very easy to put one's trust in the pot. The pot represents our comfort zone. Our comfort zone consists of all that is familiar, which includes friendships, our place of employment, church relationships, social activities and things that make up our customary way of life. This pot holds us secure and provides for us a base, a foundation for our life. All of our attitudes towards life, our belief system, values, goals and motivations are in this pot. The sad thing that most people never realize is that the pot is only an illusion. Many times those things become an invisible barrier that restricts us from pursuing the dream God has purposed for our lives. We tend to get disillusioned when we put our confidence in the things that represent our security. That could be people, a job, a financial portfolio, investments, or a variety of other things, but our real security comes from placing our confidence in God. We may even feel that we have placed our trust in God, until He allows us to lose all of those things. That is when we can take an honest inventory of our heart and acknowledge where we have difficulty trusting God. He already knows those things exist, but it becomes important for us to recognize that our faith has been anchored in the wrong things, repent, and choose to believe in His promises.

In the midst of my journey, I realized that I still had trust issues. I looked to my degree from Bible college and ordination papers as my source of confidence to open doors. I felt the conviction that the Lord wanted me to burn my ordination papers. I'm not telling others to do the same thing unless God leads them into it. That was a personal moment between me and the Lord. It wasn't meant as a sign of disrespect to those that are ordained or the organizations that offer those credentials. My wife and I have since been ordained again through a different organization, but for me at that time, it was an act of faith and obedience. I realized those things were not the things God wanted to use to open doors or validate my credibility. God doesn't need our degrees, certificates or various forms of credentials that we hold in high esteem in order for Him to do what He wants to do. The anointing is what gives a person credibility, and the testimonies of a person's journey. It is God who gives authority and it is God who ordains. When God sends a man or woman of His choosing, He has already prepared those to whom He is sending to hear the message. We need not fear our 'lack of credentials.' Those that are led by the Spirit and hear from God will recognize the confirming approval of the Holy Spirit upon His servants. There are many things the Holy Spirit may ask us to do as an act of obedience and faith. My confidence had to be settled in the fact that God is for me, and at the right time He would open the right doors.

If we put our confidence in others they may eventually disappoint us. I don't think anyone has a desire to let others down, but we are only human and it is a fact of life. People make mistakes and others will feel let down by us from time to time. If our confidence is in anything but God, people will get angry or offended when the illusion breaks apart. They may doubt their ability to trust God, thinking He has failed them. It is so important that we deal with our offenses and stop looking for someone to blame for our disappointments. God has a great track record of success stories. He doesn't fail us. We fail Him by neglecting to put our confidence in Him. God's love, His mercy, and His faithfulness endure forever. He has proven time and time again throughout history and to me personally that He is trustworthy.

Many people are stuck in a land that is all too familiar and predictable. When we have grown comfortable with our confinements, no matter how unhealthy they may be, it is a very difficult thing to make changes to our lives. It can be a scary thing to try to change jobs, career paths, drop unhealthy friendships, relocate or a variety of other things that will bring a breaking to our pot. We think of all our obligations, the fear of change, and we hear the many voices of fear and negativity that tell us we must remain where we are. Others around us will probably not feel comfortable with certain decisions we make, nor will they understand. They are not meant to. That is part of the test. How people respond to the things they don't understand is one of the tests God brings to our lives, no matter what side of the situation we're in. If it concerns our personal life, then we must be assured that we are hearing from God and making decisions based on the leading of His Spirit and His counsel. If we live our life by the leading of others or their expectations we will always be in fluctuation, a ship tossed to and fro on the waves, never reaching our destination. If it is a matter regarding someone else's life and does not require us to make a decision regarding our own personal life, it is best to stay neutral and refrain from making any critical judgments. The temptation of our flesh is to judge matters by our natural senses (what we can see or hear), but Jesus warned us not to judge for a reason. Not only are we unqualified to judge others, but there is always more to a situation than what we think we know. Only

ROOM TO GROW

God can see into a person's heart and life to know the complete picture. He knows the intent of people's heart and what motivates their actions, but others often cannot discern those things. The reality is, we cannot understand the complexities of any person's life other than our own. As much as we would not want anyone to judge or condemn us, neither should we judge others. I have had numerous opportunities to feel offended with people who gave me unsolicited religious advice or negative opinions but didn't have the mind of the Spirit. Transition is hard enough without adding unnecessary pain through negative conversation or condemnation. Transition can give us many opportunities to exercise maturity in our responses and choose forgiveness over harboring a grudge. We must also learn to exercise restraint when it comes to our words.

There are many well-meaning people who will speak words of caution, words of advice, sometimes even disguising the voice of criticism, guilt or condemnation, suggesting they know God's will for your life better than you do. It is easy for others to make demands or give advice when they don't have to live someone else's life. The problem with this is not everyone has prayed through and gotten the mind of the Lord on the issue before they speak. It is important to discern when others are speaking from their own heart and their own perspective without inspired revelation, or understanding that comes from the Holy Spirit through prayer. Others may have mixed motives for their counsel.

It takes courage to walk away and begin something new, but God does not call us to tolerate things that take us into captivity. Jesus came to set the captives free. True repentance is to take steps of faith towards God and cut off the things that prevent us from walking out our calling and fulfilling our destiny. Although I agree there are times when we must seek godly counsel, there are also times when we must take the issues of our life and trust in Him alone. God may not speak to others about the decisions concerning your life because you need to hear from God for yourself. If you are hungering after God and want the life He has for you, then you must trust Him to lead you. The Lord will help you make the changes that are necessary to move you into His desired destination. If you are not growing and thriving in your current environment, ask the Lord if He has a new environment for you. The reality is, people often don't like change and will not willingly make the hard decisions, such as leaving behind old friends or familiar routines in order to create space for new opportunities. Only the Lord knows what it will take to keep us moving along into the plans and purposes He has for us. God may simply show up in your life one day, shatter your pot, and leave you open and vulnerable to trust Him like never before.

When that container is broken, your first impulse will probably be a desperate attempt to try and figure out how to put things back in order. You may face a variety of difficult circumstances. Perhaps the job you trusted is no longer there. Maybe it's a spouse that is no longer in your life. You may find that God terminates certain relationships and friends suddenly reject you, family may voice their concerns about circumstances in your life and try to influence your decisions. The relationships that you found your identity in and fed your ego are suddenly gone. You might not even have a firm grasp on your own identity at this point. Bridges can be burned, doors shut, and it feels like a bomb went off. Pieces of your life are fragmented as you scramble for some resemblance of order. It may feel like the enemy has blindsided you, but even if he did, God will use the broken pieces of our lives to lead you in a new direction. Don't give in to pretense and pride that tells you to convince others that everything is fine, because they won't know how to help if God asks them to help you. In reality, when we find that God is pulling us up by the roots, we are experiencing a form of shock, just like a plant that has suddenly been pulled out of its container. When we go through a major life transition such as starting a new job, moving to a new city, or ending a relationship, we are uprooted from our familiar surroundings and must adapt to new circumstances. We feel uncomfortable, vulnerable, exposed and it's an awkward place to be as our mind tells us everything is far from fine. This process can be stressful, but we must adjust to our new environment so that we can continue to grow and thrive.

Why do we try to replant ourselves in the things God has obviously decided are no longer good for us? I guess for the same reasons why a person stays in that dead end job or a relationship that isn't God's best for them. No matter how unhealthy it may be it's what we know, and what we know feels safer than the unknown. There could be any number of reasons why people allow their fears to rule over their decisions, but fear of change is a compelling force that makes people afraid to leave their comfort zone.

Have you ever tried to bring a withered, dying plant back to life? You know it's too far gone to salvage but you try anyway. That plant hasn't been watered in months; it's got one shriveled up, miserable looking leaf on it and somehow we think a cup of water might do the trick to revive it. It's a laughable idea, really, but there are times when we do seem to want to keep things alive that have lost their life a long time ago. People do the same things with church programs and ministries. I did it for a long time, too. So, why are we content to drag around a dead horse and hope no one notices? Why do we fear admitting to ourselves and others when something has died, hoping no one notices? Give that dead thing a graceful funeral and position yourself for something new! Don't continue to prop up those things that are withered and dying just to give yourself or others a sense of security or because you're afraid to admit when something isn't working. If there is no movement of the Holy Spirit on it and it's not producing fruit, it has declined into a fruitless fig tree. If it has a form of godliness without the power of God, let it go! How many times has God tried to get our attention, wanting to give us a new plan and a new direction, but we are intent on doing the same old thing we've always done? Those things are weights that will detract from our ability to be fruitful and weigh us down. The anointing must be channeled in the direction God has purposed for our lives. He knows the exact location where we will receive what we need to thrive. The question is, "Will you trust Him?" Our fears must be confronted so that we can discover whether or not we are building on wood, stubble or hay. We must each find out if what we have been building is built upon the firm foundation of Jesus Christ, or if we have built upon the slippery slope of sand.

"Therefore, everyone who hears these words of mine and puts them into practice is like a wise man who built his house on the rock. The rain came down, the streams rose, and the winds blew and beat against that house; yet it did not fall, because it had its foundation on the rock. But everyone who hears these words of mine and does not put them into practice is like a foolish man who built his house on sand. The rain came down and the wind blew and beat against that house, and it fell with a great crash." (Matthew 7:24-27)

Whether or not we survive the storms of life, the shattering of our pot, is determined by where we have built our foundation. Jesus is the chief cornerstone. His plan is to shatter our man-made pots and plant us into a spacious place. I love what the Psalmist wrote in Psalms 18:19. "He brought me out into a spacious place. He rescued me because He delighted in me." I am so thankful that we can find favor with God. He is our rescuer and deliverer. Even when our foundation has been built on shaky ground, He is our safe refuge. He is able to give us the grace to make us stand.

What brings about the conditions for our deliverance? Let's take a look at Elijah in 1 Kings 17: 1-4. After declaring to Ahab there would be neither rain or dew for the next few years, the Lord spoke and said, "Leave *here* and hide in the Karith Ravine," which was also known as the Brook Cherith. "The ravens will feed you *there*." Cherith means to cut, or a place of cutting or covenant making. This same word is used when God made a covenant with Abraham. The famine not only produced judgment on Ahab's house, it brought Elijah to a place of cutting away the old mindset. It was a covenant of change.

God sent an unclean bird to feed Elijah by the brook. That wasn't easy for a man like Elijah to comprehend. He was a man that lived by the law. The law prohibited him from touching anything from the mouth of a scavenger bird. Can you just imagine the reaction of Elijah when God told him to eat what an unclean bird brought him to dine on? Do you know what scavenger birds eat? Somehow I just don't think roadkill was his choice of top menu selections. It certainly was not the diet Elijah would have chosen for himself! But, that's the point. Elijah didn't get to choose the way his provision would come, and neither do we. God chose that particular method of provision for Elijah in order to humble him and change the nature of His servant. Similarly, when we are going through a major life transition, God prepares for us a network of new relationships that will provide us with emotional, spiritual and practical support we need to succeed. It may not be what we want, but it will be what God knows we need.

Elijah really only had one choice: eat of that provision or starve. There was a famine in the land. Sometimes God has to get us in a very vulnerable place where we're hungry enough to eat the very life that will sustain us. The Bible tells us that Jesus is the Bread of Life. "If anyone eats of this bread, he will live forever," (John 6:51). In the eyes of the religious, Jesus was sharing defiled teaching. "Unless you eat of the flesh of the son of man and drink his blood, you have no life in you," (John 6:53). The disciples said, "This is hard teaching…who can accept it?" Jesus asked them if it offended them. Then He told them that the Spirit gives life and the flesh counts for nothing. "…the words I have spoken to you are Spirit and they are life," (John 6:61, 63). Only those who are willing to let Jesus offend their religious beliefs and attitudes, and be changed by the Spirit have real life. Elijah was such a man. God took Elijah out of the letter of the law, out of religious limitations in his belief system, and into a relationship where his faith could grow. Relationships, however, require trust and Elijah was about to learn a whole lot about his relationship with God.

God transplanted Elijah from the *'here'* of the natural to the *'there'* of His Spirit. How do we get there? To quote Dr. Phillips, "***There*** is where you go when ***'here'*** becomes intolerable." It became intolerable for the children of Israel in Egypt. The Israelites were fruitful and multiplied greatly, becoming exceedingly numerous so the land was filled with them. The Egyptians felt threatened by them so they oppressed the Israelites and put them under very hard bondage. The more they were oppressed, the more they multiplied. They yearned for freedom, and in anguish of heart they cried out to God for deliverance. If we let God's dream touch our hearts, it will put a hunger in us that will cause us to groan with anguish until we break free. The duties and traditions of a religious system, or a belief system marked by limitations, will always constrict the hunger and desire to fulfill God's dream. God loves us so much that He doesn't want us to stay in a constricted place. He is faithful to come and cause our heart to grow and yearn for Him. It's that hunger and desire that God responds to, and He will send the instruments of change to shatter the pot of our confinement. The Lord said to Moses, "I have indeed seen the misery of My people in Egypt. I have heard them crying out because of their slave drivers and I am concerned about their suffering. So, I have come down to rescue them from the hand of the Egyptians and to bring them up out of that land into a good and spacious land,"(Exodus 3:7-8).

Are you faced with an intolerable situation? God may be sending His instruments of change to your life even now. What you believe about your situation affects how you view God and His ability to set you free. If you feel there is no alternative available to you or that you are destined to live with your hands tied, unable to break free, that will become your reality. If, however, you choose to believe that anything is possible with God, then that belief changes how you think your story will end. It opens up a world of new opportunities without limitations, where God is free to change the course of history for your life, even the course that you may feel has already been written.

Limiting Beliefs

Some people live under self-imposed limitations such as condemnation, self-righteousness, self-rejection, a sense of unworthiness, woundedness, and unforgiveness. Negative mindsets convince people that they are unable to obtain a life of fullness for a variety of reasons. These things limit a person's ability to grow in the knowledge of Christ.

"So then, just as you received Christ Jesus as Lord, continue to live your lives in Him, rooted and built up in Him, strengthened in the faith as you were taught, and overflowing with thankfulness. See to it that no one takes you captive through hollow and deceptive philosophy, which depends on human tradition and the elemental spiritual forces of this world rather than on Christ," (Colossians 2:6-8)

There are also family imposed limitations. These are negative messages imprinted at a young age during a person's formative years. They are the messages that come from parents and other family members as they speak into your life. Parental expectations tell us what we can or cannot become in life or what we are expected to become. Parental judgments and comments tell us early on whether or not we should believe in ourselves or feel self-conscious and insecure about our identity.

Generational imposed limitations are things that are brought down into families from one generation to another. There could be genetically inherited physical ailments, disease or handicaps. There can also be inherited mindsets influenced by religious affiliation, cults, or unbelieving family members that pass down faulty beliefs from one generation to another. All of these things limit a person's ability to grow in faith or relationship with God.

A generational curse attributes negative consequences or patterns of behavior that are handed down through generations in a family. They are passed down family lines much like spiritual genetics. There are spirits that work in families to reproduce curses that are passed down from one family member to another. Past sins, transgressions, mistakes and behavior patterns can have a lasting effect on future generations. A history of poverty, addictions, divorce, untimely death, physical diseases and spiritual ailments may be attributed to a generational curse. Unbroken curses hinders a person's ability to prosper and experience more of God by producing repeated cycles of loss. These things serve to create a sense of hopelessness, unbelief and disappointment in God, and they undermine a person's ability to see God's greatness or His ability to change their situation. This can lead people to a sense of despair and

12

helplessness, but God can set us free from such things because He is the deliverer in our lives. No situation is hopeless when we have Jesus as the anchor of our hope.

Spiritually imposed limitations come from religious beliefs, ecclesiastical traditions and restrictions that tell a person how far they can go or grow within the confines of the four walls of the church. People are sometimes told things like, "That is not your calling or gifting." They might be told they are not qualified for various reasons. This only brings discouragement. How often people look for a place to serve or be promoted within the local church only to be told there's no room at the inn. So, how does a person grow and become fruitful when all the life groups have leaders, the worship teams are full, and no one is accepting applications for new pastors, teachers, ushers, greeters or child care workers? What if you don't feel called to serve within a local church body, but somewhere in the community? What if your place of service and how the anointing flows in your life is outside the church and you're not sure how to identify your place of service?

Everyone needs help identifying their spiritual gifts and place of calling. When people don't have answers to those questions, they eventually lose their passion and become quiet pew sitters. They become more interested in their position in the church than finding their place in the kingdom of God. Eventually, when people lose interest or desire, they fall away from organized religion, and sometimes, they continue to fall away from Christ. They begin to feel as though God has abandoned them and won't bring their dreams to pass. The problem with this is they have a church mentality and not a kingdom mentality. Some people feel that their dream or passion can only be fulfilled within the church, instead of trusting God to open doors in new, unexpected places.

There are many factors that can compel people to want to minister to others. Many people have experienced hardship, challenge, injustice, or inequality, and that firsthand experience motivates them to work towards change as a way to prevent others from experiencing the same type of difficulties. Others may feel a strong call towards social justice issues such as environmentalism, human rights, or a particular cause. They are driven by a deep desire to make a positive difference in the world. People who have a strong sense of empathy and compassion may be called to serve in yet other areas of mercy ministries, and still others may use their creative talents and abilities to bring beauty through art, music, or come up with innovative solutions to bring about change in other areas. Explore your interests and passions. Pursue the things that make you feel fulfilled. Overall, there are a multitude of ways that people can serve in the Kingdom of God.

God wants to challenge limited mindsets that cause people to feel that pastors and leaders fail to recognize their spiritual gifts or give them a place in the local church to exercise those gifts. Many people end up feeling slighted or offended with leadership because they seek recognition or a place of importance, but can't find it within their local church. This is an unrealistic expectation to place upon pastors and leaders. There are limited positions within any local church, but there is never a lack of opportunity in the Kingdom of God. Opportunities abound in the open field of God's kingdom, so stop banging on the closed door, and open your eyes to see the door that is standing open.

There are multitudes that have decided not to participate in church for various reasons. Some aren't satisfied with what they find in their local churches, but they still love Jesus and would love to have fellowship, teaching, and worship with other Christians. Particularly in this younger generation, I believe they are seeking what they feel is authentic Christianity. They are scrutinizing those that claim to be Christians and looking for good fruit. They genuinely desire the real Jesus, but they don't have any interest in pretense or what they consider fake Christianity. Now perhaps more than ever, the church must bear the fruit worthy of repentance or we will fail to reach the multitudes that still need Jesus.

Finding the right church, home fellowship or the tribe of people that resonates with you can take time. The reality is sometimes you don't fit and it feels like you're a fish out of water, or trying to make a square peg fit into a round hole. It is frustrating trying to find that place where you try to fit in and it just doesn't feel right. God doesn't make us to be like everyone else. He makes us uniquely different in order to become salt and light, an influence to others around us. Don't worry if you don't fit. It doesn't mean you've done anything wrong. It just means you haven't found the right place yet. God probably has you in a season of growth where He is preparing you to find your place a little later down the road, and that's ok. He may be refining trust issues or working on developing your spiritual hearing without the benefit of leaning on others. Those with prophetic anointing especially may find themselves alone with God or having a cave experience for an extended period of time. This is where we learn humility and dependence on God. We have gone through seasons of belonging to a church family and enjoying those relationships, but we have also gone through seasons where we didn't have that. During the years we lived in Pensacola, we had a long season of belonging to one particular church. Then, one day, God broke us out of the box and we started a street ministry. After that, we felt like we just didn't fit inside the box the same way anymore. Especially after we came back to California, we found difficulty finding a local church that felt like it was the right fit for our family. We wanted it, but for a very long period of time we prayed to find a local church to no avail. It seemed like God just ignored that prayer. That in itself seemed perplexing because He answered many other prayers, and it wasn't that He wasn't communicating. He just wasn't talking about that particular subject. We have found that many times the places God led us were not always about being with people that are just like us, but in fact were quite opposite; a group of believers that loved God but lacked what we supplied in areas of our gifting. So, be patient with the process. God showed us when we were to remain with a certain group of people or a particular church, and He also showed us when it was time to move on. At various times He led us to a watering hole (a local church) for a short season, but we understood when that particular season ended. Each person is unique and God's purposes are different for all of us, but Laura and I are messengers sent with a message, and we've gotten used to the fact that God directs us to release a particular message to a church or body of believers.

At one point, after a very long dry spell, we finally realized the disillusionment and dissatisfaction unchurched people experienced as they sought a place for their own families. God was also weeding out the religiousness, the guilt and feelings of self-condemnation of not being dutiful to being in a local church. No one was condemning us but our own minds. We had been trained to believe that only the rebellious didn't go to church. When your mindset has been bound by a religious spirit, the freedom we have in Christ feels awkward and somewhat uncomfortable to adjust to as we shake ourselves free from the old way of thinking. There were still beliefs left over from the past that God needed to unravel. He shattered religious misconceptions and unraveled faulty beliefs. Sometimes I think we don't really know how to walk in the freedom for which Christ has set us free. There is no condemnation for those who are in Christ, according to Romans 8:1. God affirmed His love for us, and assured us that His acceptance wasn't based on church attendance. He showed us that we could enjoy a sense of family in many houses of worship or in small group gatherings outside of a local church, and not to allow those false burdens of guilt to come upon us. We have experienced so many wonderful friendships that sometimes it was difficult choosing which house of worship we wanted to attend, because the people we loved were in different churches. We traveled from one house of worship to another, enjoying the variety of worship styles, those who brought the word of God, ministry and fellowship with our brothers and sisters in the Lord. It was a beautiful picture of loving one another and becoming one with the church in our city.

When the Lord looks at His body, He sees one church in any given city. I don't think the Lord ever intended for the walls of the church to keep His people apart or segregated from one another. Where the spirit of the Lord is, there is liberty. Pastors must learn to let go of the possessiveness they feel towards the flock, because it doesn't belong to them. They must learn to not take offense or feel insecure when people visit other churches. God may have a message in a different house they need to hear. Perhaps there is personal ministry, a prophetic word, or deliverance elsewhere that is vital to their health and well being. We should never want to deprive them of that just because we fear losing a member of the flock. Possessiveness, fear and control are indicators of idolatry. If we, as a body, continue to have this fluid motion of interconnectivity, we never have to feel a sense of loss or control. Churches will have a continual ebb and flow of people that find a place to exercise their spiritual gifts. This doesn't always have to look like the typical church. Many times this can take place in home fellowships, coffee shops, a park or any place people choose to gather in the Lord's name. We've even had some tremendous ministry in businesses and hair salons. Wherever you can gather, you can have church. This is the kingdom of God! It's how it looked in the Book of Acts. Jesus prayed to His Father in John 17 that we would be one with Him and one another. The important thing to remember is we all need one another. We need the spiritual gifts, wisdom, testimonies and experiences of others in the body of Christ. Do not forsake gathering together with others, because without one another we can never effectively build God's kingdom or share the love of God with others. We are not meant to be alone. We are designed to help meet one another's needs.

Belonging to a body of believers who are like-minded spiritually is important for individuals as it provides a sense of community, fosters spiritual growth, and offers opportunities for service and outreach. We all need a sense of belonging or contributing to something greater than ourselves. It helps give us a sense of stability. When people do not have a local church or a support system of other Christians, it can feel very lonely. This is when the enemy strikes, because we are vulnerable when we are isolated and alone. When people feel disconnected and dissatisfied, they are vulnerable to a whole host of lies. It's important to discern when the enemy is feeding us lies because if we can't distinguish how Satan tries to manipulate us, it can be very easy to end up listening to his lies and getting angry with God. This can lead to backsliding, disinterest towards the things of the Spirit, and feelings that try to tell us that God just doesn't care about us. Without revelation, the temptation is for people to cast off restraint and go back to living without Christ being fully involved in their life. It is hard to go through darkness when we don't understand how to navigate our course, but keep in mind that God hasn't left, even when He's silent. Many Christians go through fiery trials and sometimes things don't turn out the way we hope, but there is comfort in knowing that He is there as we go through challenges. God doesn't promise we won't experience adversity and hardship; those things come to everyone, but our faith can still be strong in the midst of it, knowing that every test or trial has an expiration date. Although at

15

times it may feel like God has abandoned us, that is not the truth. God's promise to us in Hebrews 13:5 is that He will never leave us or forsake us. All of the lies, misconceptions and negative emotions must be challenged or they become spiritually imposed limitations to our faith. If a person finds themselves in this sort of situation they will remain stuck. Prophecy God's promises until you get to the other side of the storm! Challenge every lie of unbelief so that you can change what you believe.

The belief system of an individual can also be significantly influenced and limited by both environmental and cultural factors, which shapes their perspective and attitudes towards the world. Environmental factors include things like physical surroundings. Some people feel trapped in difficult family situations that make them feel as though certain situations will never change. Sometimes situations don't change until we take specific action, but instead of admitting we're afraid to take a step of faith, our fears tell us we are trapped and a victim of our circumstances. What is it that's really stopping you? If you examine what you believe to be true, the answer is often within yourself rather than the actual circumstances. Victims find it easier to blame others rather than take responsibility for their life. So, how do you benefit by holding on to your current beliefs? These are tough questions but if you are willing to confront these negative beliefs within yourself, you can push through the self-doubt and paralysis that stops you from making important changes.

Cultural factors also play a significant role in shaping a person's belief system. Cultural norms, values, and traditions often dictate what is acceptable or unacceptable behavior, which also influences a person's beliefs and attitudes. For example, in some cultures, it may be considered taboo to question authority or challenge traditional beliefs. This can limit a person's ability to think critically and form their own unique beliefs. This can affect a person's ability to empathize with others who hold different beliefs. This can also lead to a lack of understanding and tolerance towards those who hold different opinions, which ultimately leads to limiting the individual's ability to learn and grow from diverse perspectives. People have no choice as to their sex, race, social status or geography where they are born. Many people might say, "Well, if I had just been born a different color," or, "If I just lived in a different neighborhood or country, my life would be a lot different." One could say, "If I wasn't born a minority, a woman, or if I just had the opportunity to have a better education, my life would be so much better." "If I didn't have to work this minimum wage job…" "If I wasn't a single mom…" "If I didn't have this physical handicap…" But where does it end? We can all come up with excuses when we don't have the answers to overcoming obstacles. The real question to ask ourselves is why we tell ourselves stories that disempower us. It's what you believe to be true about your current situation that makes you feel stuck. When challenges and situations feel impossible, we all tend to focus on what we see as limitations. It's not to say people don't have real life challenges, and certainly this is not meant to minimize anyone's struggle in life. However, every one of those limiting thoughts are tied into a mindset of unbelief that tries to convince us that change is too difficult or altogether impossible. Instead, focus on what you do have control of and make choices that put you back in the driver's seat of your life. Ask the Holy Spirit for a different perspective so you can see new possibilities on how to approach your problem.

Religious beliefs are often deeply ingrained and passed down through generations, which can make it difficult for individuals to challenge or question them. This can lead to a person whose mind is closed to new ideas that conflict with how they have been raised. Religious doctrines and teachings can also be interpreted in a variety of ways,

16

which can lead to differing beliefs among individuals who share the same faith. There are often lifestyle restrictions that come with certain faiths and beliefs that further limit a person's ability to explore and experience life. These differences can create divisions within religious communities and limit the potential for the growth of their faith and understanding.

It is not our responsibility to figure out how God will answer our prayers, only to believe that He is greater than the problems and situations that place limits upon our lives. We really must decide if the God we believe in is big enough to handle our problems, and whether or not we will choose to trust Him to take the wheel and redirect our life.

Sometimes it is very difficult to realize our need for deliverance. All we know and understand is what we have experienced. Our minds are conditioned to accept the environment to which we have grown accustomed. I grew up in church and was taught that church was my refuge. It was a source of safety and peace. The world was dark and unsafe, and it was reinforced in my mind that it wasn't safe outside the camp. Religious attitudes can be very exclusive and can cause people to develop an *us* vs. *them* mentality. This leads to judgmentalism and legalism towards others. It is interesting to me that Jesus was crucified outside the camp. The religious didn't consider Him worthy of the temple because they didn't accept Him. He came to His own people but they didn't receive Him either.

While church can be a very comforting place, the truth is, it is the Lord that is our refuge, not a brick and mortar building. Jesus is our strong tower. He is a mighty fortress, our strength and our shield. Over and over again in scripture we see the storms but we also see Jesus as the one we must run to. "God is our refuge and strength. A very present help in trouble," (Psalm 46:1).

When I was younger I struggled to be accepted by my peers and mentors. I wanted so much for them to see my faithfulness to the duties and responsibilities to the church, but the more I tried to please men with my religious observances, the weaker I felt. It was like it drained the very life out of me. I was trying to serve people in hopes that it pleased God, but I had it backwards. I should have served God because of my love for Him first, and allowed Him to love me, then love others through my service. It was a lesson I needed to learn because it choked the life of the Spirit out of me. My spirit withered and my faith was bound by lack of joy, resulting in a lack of fruit in my life and ministry. God allowed me to fail in every area of my life so I would be totally humbled, because I had already been blinded. I needed Him to lead me and deliver me. After being in the pastorate for many years, I needed my Savior more than ever. When I resigned, I left behind 25 years of friendships, family, service and ministry connections.

My emotions went from one extreme to another. As I experienced freedom from my bondage, my emotions overwhelmed me. I felt the incredible rush of adrenaline, and an incredible joy. I felt like a thousand pounds had been taken off my shoulders. I also felt incredible shame, loneliness and separation. None of it was handled the way I had hoped, and the enemy had also been involved to magnify offenses, gossip, and escalate the situation. I was amazed at how quickly and easily the people I had loved and served for many years turned their backs and rejected me, but they also did not understand my reasons for leaving. They were hurt, I was hurt, but I understood later it was the Lord that made sure those doors were closed. He had a new purpose and direction for my life. Sometimes we don't understand why our bridges seem to be burned beyond repair, but the Lord knows how to make sure we don't go back to what's ordinary or familiar. When He wants to move us into our future we will find doors closed so that we are forced to look outside our comfort zone. Others will not have the ear to hear what God is speaking to you. Others will not have the faith to walk through what God is asking of you. It is a hard thing to endure rejection or criticism for wanting more for your life, but God is so faithful to comfort us when others have rejected us. We cannot live trying to please everyone. Live to please God, and He will take care of the rest.

Transition periods in life can be challenging for many people, as they often involve significant changes that can be difficult to navigate. It is normal to experience uncertainty about the future. This can feel very unsettling and may lead to feelings of anxiety or fear. Transitions often include letting go of something that was important or familiar, such as a job, a relationship, a home or significant people. This can cause grief and sadness, but let yourself go through the grief process. It is important to be honest with the Lord about everything you're feeling so that He can heal you. Transitions can also challenge our sense of identity, as we learn that who we are is not tied to what we do. This can be especially difficult if our sense of identity is tied to the thing we are letting go of. We belong to our Father, and our identity and security is anchored on our relationship with Him. Transitions can feel very lonely as we leave behind support networks and try to build new ones. We find ourselves in isolation even if it is for a short time. Transitions can be difficult, but they are also opportunities for growth and self-discovery.

I spent many nights crying to the Lord. I ran to Him the only way I knew how, through a repentant and grateful heart. God broke me free and I praised Him for it. I had no idea what God was going to do next, but I knew that passion was once again restored to my life. I felt alive again! His presence in my daily life became more important than His presence in church. His promises for my life became more important than the countless number of sermons I worked on to feed others. My fellowship with the Holy Spirit became more important than the fellowship with others. He is the great "I Am!" Jesus is the Bread of Life. He is the light and the life we need. "The righteous cry out and the Lord hears them. He delivers them from all their troubles," (Psalm 34:17). I am so thankful for my God who delivers. He answered the cry of my heart for more of Him. God is able to deliver anyone who desires to see His dream come to pass in their life. But, please be warned - He may need to break your pot!

Prayer to Trust God During Transition

Dear Heavenly Father,

As I stand at the crossroads of this new chapter in my life, I come to You with a humble heart, seeking Your guidance and direction. I know that You are the only one who can provide me with the strength and wisdom that I need to navigate this time of transition.

Lord, I ask for Your grace and mercy to be upon me as I step into the unknown. I pray that You would fill me with Your peace that surpasses all understanding, and that You would calm any fears or anxieties that I may have.

Please give me the courage to face any challenges that may arise, and help me to trust in Your plan for my life. I know that You have good plans and a good future for me, so I ask that You help me stay focused on Your will for me, even when it doesn't make sense.

Thank you for Your unfailing love and faithfulness to me, even in the midst of uncertain times. I trust in Your provision and care, and I pray that You lead me forward with confidence and hope. Please lead me to those You have chosen to provide for me and open new doors of opportunity. In Jesus' name, amen.

ROOM TO GROW

CHAPTER TWO
Driving Out the Enemy

"You transplanted a vine out of Egypt; You drove out the nations and planted it. You cleared the ground for it, and it took root and filled the land." Psalm 80:8,9

Many people find themselves uprooted from ministries, family, friends, and cities for a variety of reasons. Some are personal choices we make for ourselves and others feel compelled to leave for one reason or another. During times of stress, it is so difficult to see the hand of God at work. God knows His dream for us is bigger than the pot we are planted in, but sometimes we are blind to our need for relocation. God pries us from our pot by bringing circumstances beyond our control. Many times, we suddenly find ourselves in the midst of trouble and do not realize that it's the answer to our prayers for more of Him. Perhaps a situation has been contrived by the enemy to plot your failure, or perhaps you've been mistreated, rejected, fired or displaced for reasons you might not easily explain. When the enemy gets involved in making a mess of your life, it can get very, very complicated and difficult to make anyone else truly understand there are spiritual dynamics involved, especially if others are not Christians. Motives are often hidden, and while the spiritual part of you understands the deception and evil scheming of the enemy, trying to explain those sort of things to someone else, especially if it's a potential new employer or others outside of that situation, often leaves you sounding slightly unbalanced or like a conspiracy nut. Sometimes there is no way to make bad things sound like there is a good reason why those things happened. You can't make others understand what you've gone through. They won't understand and you would probably sound worse for trying. You may be misunderstood, gossiped about or your name slandered. In this day and age of cancel culture, many people simply don't know how to recover from a severely damaged reputation. You may find yourself facing a variety of other challenges.

What's worse is when the Lord tells you to not even try to defend yourself and keep your mouth shut while everyone else is busy tearing you down. An enormous conflict takes place in your soul as you wonder how you can get through each day and make something new out of your life. You wonder how long it's going to hurt and you question the extent of what else it will cost you to follow your dream. I think Joseph had those same questions, too.

Joseph went through several transitions in his life, including being sold into slavery by his jealous brothers, being falsely accused of a crime and thrown into prison, and ultimately being appointed as second-in-command to

Pharaoh in Egypt, (Genesis 37-50). Before Joseph was ready for promotion into God's higher purposes, he endured the crucible of God's prison. No matter how much Joseph wanted his freedom, it would not change God's mind, because what God was going for was Joseph's complete surrender. God was in the midst of maturing and transforming Joseph into a new man. Joseph wasn't just a slave in Potifer's house, he was in the prison, but even in prison, God gave him favor.

Freedom from slavery was an ideal offer for the children of Israel. They were to be released from 430 years of oppression. Nothing mattered but having a picture of the ideal, the fulfillment of God's promise. Oh, to live in the land of promise that they had heard so much about growing up! It was to be a land flowing with milk and honey, rich in abundance. Each family would have his own home and property, homes and farms they would not need to build. That ideal picture, one of initial joy and adulation from deliverance, was quickly tempered three days later. An impassable road lay before them and the armies of Egypt were behind them. They were completely hemmed in with no place to go. The excitement soon became diffused with reality. The thoughts of being completely destroyed went through their minds like the familiar cries that were trumpeted in Moses' ears. "Was it because there were no graves in Egypt that you brought us to the desert to die?" (Exodus 14:11,12). The taunts were similar to the railings that were thrown at Jesus. His enemies said, "He saved others; let Him save Himself, if He is the Christ of God, the chosen one…" the soldiers said. "If you are the King of the Jews, save yourself," (Luke 23:35). This is the temptation of the wilderness, as Jesus understood quite well. Do anything to try to save yourself instead of yielding to the plan of God and choosing His will instead of your own.

It was a three day journey from the exodus from Egypt to the Red Sea. The miraculous signs and wonders that they gloried in were seemingly forgotten in the reality that they might die stuck in the wilderness. Here was an insurmountable test of faith, a point of no return. They were faced with the decision to give their lives wholly to God and trust Him completely or perish in their unbelief. I am sure many of them considered striking a deal with Pharaoh to get their old jobs back. They could have explained that they had a moment of temporary insanity to follow a rebel like Moses. They could have shown their eagerness by pledging allegiance to Pharaoh and killing Moses. They were a people driven by fear and uncertainty. Moses was God's chosen leader to bring His people out of bondage and into freedom. Many years earlier, Moses experienced a transition of his own when he killed an Egyptian and he hid in the desert. There were many years of learning how to hear God's voice and walk in humility so that one day Moses would be ready to lead God's people out of bondage and into freedom. When God wants to do a deep work of preparation in a person's life, it begins in obscurity, where He hides His work from the enemy in order to preserve the individual for His greater purposes. God had a plan to bless His people and show His glory, and nobody would thwart that plan.

Moses was also a dreamer. He had a love and desire to serve God, and most importantly, to know God. Others were afraid of Him and shrunk back from any personal relationship with the awesome Jehovah, but Moses had an insatiable desire for the presence of God. He had an awe and wonder about the great "I AM" that he had encountered in the burning bush. Others were content to experience the signs and wonders of His power, but Moses sought to know Him in a face-to-face relationship. Who was this God that put His God sized dreams in his heart? Who was *he* that God would choose him to carry out such an important responsibility? Didn't God know that Moses didn't feel like much of a leader? Certainly He understood that he wasn't very good at public speaking, and tended to

22

stumble over his words, especially when he felt nervous. Didn't God know about his past? There were failures there - *big ones.* Why would anyone listen to him or take him seriously? Nevertheless, God's dream was lodged so deep in his heart that Moses couldn't deny it existed. God's dream became a compass that continued to steer him in the direction of his destiny. It took some time for Moses to understand God's criteria for choosing his leaders. Later, he realized that he was exactly the type of man God wanted; a person that didn't think too highly of himself and would follow God's lead in everything He asked.

"I am the Lord; that is my name. I will not give my glory to anyone else or the praise I deserve to idols," (Isaiah 42:8, God's Word Translation). "Instead, God chooses things the world considers foolish in order to shame those who think they are wise. And He chooses things that are powerless to shame those who are powerful," (1 Corinthians 1:27).

Some people have such a hard time seeing other people's dreams fulfilled. Dreamers always seem to attract the dream killers. They're the critics that shoot down your dreams, the mockers that make you feel foolish for entertaining such wonderful possibilities in your heart. Dream killers are people who once had dreams in their heart, but allowed them to die in unbelief. They are the ones who have grown bitter and disillusioned with God. Dream killers are like those that throw cold water on the hopes of others; they don't want to be reminded of someone else's dream because they are prisoners of hopelessness. Prisoners despise the freedom of others. As with the story of Joseph, the dream killers always seem to think it's a reasonable option to kill the dream or kill off the dreamer in order to maintain their status in life and feel better about themselves.

Joseph's brothers were full of jealousy. Joseph was having encounters with God which was evident through his dreams and the revelation he received. God showed Joseph pieces of his future which his brothers despised. When someone is having supernatural encounters with God and others are not, it can create jealousy. Eventually, the brothers' jealousy grew to the point where they couldn't wait to get rid of him. Jealousy is fear that someone you see as a rival may enjoy a benefit or some advantage that you desire for yourself. A jealous person would probably never admit they have those awkward, uncomfortable feelings, but the wilderness has a way of causing those petty insecurities to surface. God waits until we understand we are not getting out of the wilderness until those character issues are firmly dealt with and eradicated from our heart. Jealousy is a root system that will cause people to sin with their mouths and speak negatively against others. God equates character assassination with murder, and He will not promote someone with such darkness in their heart.

Jealousy is an emotion that can come from broken covenants, betrayal, broken promises, fear or insecurity, and it can be inherited as a generational root. It can be planted in a person's heart as a seed that comes as a result of fear, insecurity, rejection or offense. When a person feels insecure about their identity, they fail to understand their position of favor simply because of their relationship with their heavenly Father. If you have asked God to forgive your sins, and have invited Jesus to be Your Lord and Savior, you are adopted into the family of God as His child. You can enjoy the same benefits that are available to Jesus and any other children of God. Jealousy creates an underlying insecurity that causes a person to feel slighted, offended or resentful that they will be overlooked. They are afraid someone else will receive a blessing that they may not receive for themselves. A person battling jealous feelings may withdraw when those feelings arise. They find it difficult to offer compliments, congratulatory comments, praise,

23

or genuinely feel happy for others because a spirit of competition sees others as rivals. Sometimes those pent up feelings cause people to fire off belittling remarks or other negative comments that aim to strip all joy from others. The important thing to realize is that jealousy is another limited mindset that comes from disobedience and unbelief. Biblical examples are found in the lives of Saul, who resented David and tried to kill his up and coming successor; Cain, who killed his brother Abel, and Jezebel, who conspired against and killed Naboth to seize his vineyard.

All of these people were examples of unrestrained jealousy, and all of them had murder in their heart. Jealousy causes anger, resentment, and results in evil imaginations. They see others as rivals that stand between themselves and something they want for themselves. Joseph's brothers were full of jealousy. They resented Joseph's close relationship to their father and the way he favored Joseph. The brothers resented his big dreams and didn't want to hear about them. Joseph's dreams represented a humbling coming to their lives and a promotion coming to Joseph. As with anyone that harbors evil in their heart, the enemy was with them to create the long awaited opportunity to rid themselves of this dreamer. They threw him into a pit, left him for dead, then changed their minds and sold him to slave traders that would take him into a far off land. Joseph's brothers justified their actions to themselves that at least they would not be guilty of murder, but from a spiritual perspective, they were just as guilty. Their crime of injustice was inscribed in the books of heaven and it bore witness against them. The brothers destroyed the coat of many colors that had been a gift from their father, because it reminded them of the favor in Joseph's life. They threw goat's blood on it, tore it, and showed it to their father as 'proof' that his beloved son had been killed by wild animals and was gone forever. Each brother helped to collaborate the story they made up, never stopping for a moment to consider the grief they caused to their father. Finally, their wrath had been satisfied. They did their best to destroy any future possibility of Joseph's dreams coming true. The dreamer was gone and as good as dead. Little did they know that God would turn the tables on them many years later, and force them to need the very man they had callously rejected. They dismissed him as insignificant, but to God, Joseph was anything but insignificant.

Joseph's life is symbolic of Jesus. Joseph was falsely accused and imprisoned, just as Jesus was falsely accused and sentenced to death. Joseph interpreted dreams to reveal spiritual truth, just as Jesus performed miracles and spoke in parables to teach spiritual truths. After much suffering, Joseph was exalted to a position of power and authority in Egypt, just as Jesus was exalted to the right hand of God in heaven. Joseph's exalted position of favor was a surprise to his brothers, who thought they would never see him again, just like the resurrection of Jesus took the enemy by surprise and showed a much greater reality that had not occurred to him. Joseph's brothers did not stop to consider the pain they caused to their father, just as we often fail to understand the pain and offense we cause to our heavenly Father in the ways we treat our brothers and sisters in the Lord. Joseph endured many years of injustices as well as emotional pain that he had to submit to God and work through. Scripture doesn't elaborate much on that, but he was a man just like anyone else. I am sure that it was a difficult process to walk through to come to terms with the things that he experienced.. There is much to let go of so that we don't get stuck in the past. I wonder if Joseph asked the question that many of us do. "Where is the God of justice?" Our perspective of justice and God's perspective of justice often look quite different, and He will wait until we can agree His way is superior. God's perspective of justice often looks like forgiveness and mercy towards those that mistreated us. This is God working to form the image of Christ in us. Joseph forgave his brothers and saved them from starvation, just as Jesus forgave his enemies and saved them from eternal death. Both men endured great suffering and persecution, but ultimately triumphed over their enemies and saved their people. Joseph's life was expendable to his brothers, but never to the Lord, because God had a dream for Joseph's life that was his particular assignment. This is an important reminder that God has unique assignments for us all, and we may never understand the significance of each person fulfilling their destiny and how it may personally impact us. God doesn't show us ahead of time. If Joseph's brothers understood how greatly they would need him one day, and the fact that their very survival depended on Joseph, they wouldn't have tried to destroy him and his future. God knew the brothers would try to kill Joseph and understood the need to remove Joseph from their lives in order to preserve the plan and the dream of God.

In His message *"Change Has Come,"* TD Jakes makes an excellent point. Jakes said, "God put Joseph in a place of influence for posterity sake. He was there to influence his descendants and change the course of nature. He broke generational curses and changed the course of their lives. He was brought into a new position and a new place in life and they were all blessed because of him. The person God chose to bless them was a person they all mistreated." "Be careful how you treat folks. Especially people you think you don't need. Because God can move a person you think you don't need into a position of such power that you have to have them. And wouldn't it be good if you hadn't mistreated them when they were down so that they could think well of you when they got in power." - TD Jakes

Perhaps you feel like you can relate to Joseph's story. Perhaps you, too, have faced dream killers and now you are left feeling broken, battered, discouraged and unsure of your future. Or, maybe you're wondering how on earth God could possibly work out the impossibilities in your own life in order to fulfill the dream in your heart. Many people wonder how God can take the broken pieces of their life and put them together again. When I left my position at the church, I had no idea what I was going to do. Like Israel, I felt like my back was against the wall. I was hemmed in on all sides with no future income. I knew I was not going to look for another ministry position anytime soon, but for the most part, that was the only thing I had done for quite some time. I had overseen some project management in the church building project as well as in the flooring industry, but that was many years earlier. I applied for a variety of miscellaneous jobs but no doors opened. I kept praying, asking God to show me the one right door. Desperation can cause us to think outside the box. One day, I had an inspired idea to write to the owner of the house we were renting to see if I could somehow work off the rent. This led to consistent work, as these owners had quite a few rental properties. It showed me that God was still willing to show me favor even though I had just experienced a difficult failure. I had no one that was willing to vouch for me except God, and He was enough. He is enough for you, too. God can create the door you need. Trust Him.

Restoration takes time, and it's important to stay focused on the positive changes you are making in your life. Stay committed to taking the right actions. It is a deeply personal and spiritual process between you and your heavenly Father. It is important to remember that God is loving, kind, forgiving and compassionate. With faith and perseverance, He leads us into healing, deliverance and a new beginning.

Bruce Wilkinson wrote a wonderful fictional story called *The Dream Giver.* (Multnomah Books, 2003). It is a story about a young man named Ordinary, who lived in the land of Familiar with all the other Nobodies. He went about his life like all the other Nobodies until one morning he woke up with these words in his mind: "What you are missing you already have…" (Wilkinson, pg.14, Multnomah Books, 2003). "Could it be? Ordinary looked and looked.

And then he discovered that in a small corner of his heart lay a Big Dream." The Big Dream told him that he, a Nobody, was made to be a Somebody and destined to achieve Great Things. We are all destined to achieve great things for God, because God is a big dreamer and He's the one that puts His dreams in our heart. He wouldn't put them there if He didn't have good plans to help make those dreams come true!

Maybe you lost sight of a dream you once had. Perhaps you tried and saw your hopes dashed on the rocks of defeat. Lift up your head! It's not too late to dream again. As long as you have breath, it's never too late. You may have given up on your dream, but don't give up on the one who gave you the dream. He's the one who can help you dream again. Why don't you ask Him? The Bible says in Psalms 18:35, "You give me Your shield of victory and Your right hand sustains me; You stoop down to make me great." Isn't that an incredible thought? The Creator God of the universe is willing to stoop down to make me (and you!) great.

What Ordinary and the children of Israel needed to know in regards to fulfilling God's dream for their life is that it cost the blood of a sinless lamb. That shield of faith is Jesus, and behind that blood we have the faith to face any enemy that tries to kill our dream. Ordinary had to face many obstacles, and he had to sacrifice many things before leaving his comfort zone. The quote I love the most is when Ordinary said to himself, "There was something wonderful about nothing happening." (Wilkinson, Multnomah Books, 2003). When nothing is happening in our Christian life and we don't have to confront the enemies of the dream, the dream becomes stagnant and ceases to increase. Ordinary confronts Borderland Bullies that want to keep him in the land of Familiar, and the challenges of the wasteland. He also reaches the Valley of the Giants. Each test he courageously passes. Not because Ordinary is a Somebody, but because he serves Somebody who became a Nobody, so that he could reach his Promise Land.

Driving Out Condemnation, Rejection and Anxiety

When I resigned my position as pastor, I experienced a great attack on my mind. The enemy knew I was vulnerable and sought to bring fear, condemnation and confusion. The wilderness is a place where we are tested so that we can see what's in our heart. God already knows, but it's important for us to also recognize what's there. Some tests are to measure our integrity, our faith, or our trust in God. Others are designed to evaluate our ability to obediently wait on God and test our level of patience, and still other tests measure our ability to love others, or if we will be offended with God. These may come in different forms, such as physical, emotional, financial or spiritual, and they may vary in duration and intensity, but they are all opportunities to demonstrate our level of commitment to God. Of course, Satan is also interested because then he knows how to further tempt us, hoping we fail the wilderness tests. Would I hide behind the blood washed, Spirit anointed shield, or was I going to hide in my forms of religion, traditions and philosophies? In my heart I knew I wanted to fulfill the dream of God for my life, but I had no idea how to get there. From where I was standing, there were so many unanswered questions. We often just want to skip ahead to doing what we think we're supposed to be doing with our lives, when God isn't even speaking on those things yet. He is trying to work character and good fruit in our lives. This is where we learn to walk in blind faith. It's impossible to understand how the next steps are going to unfold. The only real comfort I had was holding on to my understanding that God was good. I knew that He never took something away without being willing to provide something better, but we never know when the 'something better' is going to show up. When a person has gone through a pot breaking experience, life as they once knew it is over. The future seemed uncertain and my dreams for God were nowhere in sight. The enemy was right there beside me, whispering in my ear all the reasons why I should have felt justified at not trusting God.

I am not a professional gardener, but I have transplanted a few plants in my time. One of the things I've noticed when taking a root-bound plant out of its pot is that the roots take the shape of the pot. They are tightly wound and gnarled. The roots have to be shaken free and the roots go through temporary shock. It's a delicate process because it's important not to destroy the root system. There are soil additives to treat root shock, but the best treatment is plenty of water. The remedy with people is very similar. We need the spiritual watering of the Holy Spirit to minister to us, to bring a revival and a refreshing. The vulnerability and exposure we feel is the shock on the roots of our belief system. God shakes the limitations and the lies of the enemy that our beliefs have placed on His dream. We must shake free from legalism, the control of religious spirits and the condemnation that plagues our mind. We must counteract every lie of unbelief and false teaching. We must battle anxious thoughts by taking the sword of the Spirit and the truth of His word. We must fight against every enemy of our faith, including shame, disgrace and humiliation that try to convince us we will not amount to anything and the dream of God is dead. We must be delivered from our pot mentality that tells us God only works within the limited scope of our understanding. God challenges us to find out what we really believe, as we find out how little we actually know about His ways. We are faced with the opportunity of getting to know the God of all our impossibilities. At times it may feel as though our life is such a complicated mess that He has to rewrite our life story, but the reality is He has already written a good plan for our lives, and every misstep, failure and plot of the enemy intended to derail us from our destiny has already been accounted for. God is never caught off guard. He makes provision for every need and has thoughtfully considered every lie and scheme of the enemy to make sure it isn't successful. God ensures the fulfillment of His dream and His promises. He is our Creator, and can always create new doors and opportunities for us regardless of our circumstances.

The first thing we must learn to do is run to Him and trust Him like never before! The blood of Jesus becomes our saving strength when we are confronted with the enemies of condemnation, shame, rejection and anxiety. I felt incredible anxiety as I sought Him for direction. I needed to extend my faith in Him for who He was as a person, as well as the comfort of His promises. God does not promise us that we will not face fear, but He does promise us that He will be with us through it. I have found God to be very faithful. He never left me and He never ceased to provide for me. He brought provision from unexpected places to bless me and strengthen my faith. He was leading me even though at the time I wasn't quite sure what I was doing. After some months went by, it seemed that God who had been in front leading me somehow disappeared. Later, I realized that He had gone behind me, closing the door on my past and those who opposed me, just as He did in Exodus 14:19. The Angel of God who had been traveling in front of Israel's army withdrew and went behind them, coming between Egypt and Israel. The glory of the Lord is our rear guard, watching out for enemies that would try to ambush us.

God withdraws for seasons in our lives to test our responses. Our faith is tested, but so is our love. Simply put, He offends our understanding of His word, and everything in our nature that dictates how we think He is supposed to act. When we think we have Him figured out, He will show us how little we understand about Him. He does things for which we have no explanation and allows situations to take unexpected turns that throw us off balance. We find that He works outside the box, way beyond our understanding. One thing we need to understand is that God is free to operate outside of our understanding and He doesn't care if it offends us! He will bring us to a point of surrender so that all we can do is allow Him to *show* us. He wants us to see the flaws in our relationship with Him and realize how imperfect our love for Him has been. He wants us to feel the desperation of needing Him to take us into a new dimension of knowing Him. The feelings of anger, frustration and offense are part of dealing with root shock.

God uses difficult circumstances of our lives to refine and shape us. The prison of His will may be a season of hardship, pain, or struggle, but it is also a place of transformation, where we learn we can rely on God and grow in our faith. Through our trials, God can drive out the enemies of shame, fear, anxiety, humiliation, and anger from our lives, replacing them with the fruits of the Spirit, such as love, joy, peace, patience, kindness, goodness, faithfulness, gentleness and self-control.

God miraculously opened a door to move to Florida. During this time, I had also gotten remarried. My wife and I had heard about the renewal services at Brownsville Assembly of God and were excited to experience the powerful presence of God in the meetings. We looked forward to the refreshing times as we traveled across the country to our new destination. The timing of the situation was a bit awkward. Due to circumstances beyond our control , we were forced to leave right about the time hurricane Ivan was making its arrival in Florida. Again, it was another test. Would we trust God in another unsettling situation? Laura was 7 months pregnant and we were driving from California to Florida right into the middle of a huge storm. We were pulling a trailer and the car was packed with 2 cats, a bird, a chihuahua and our belongings. It was a sight! We didn't know what to expect. Several other hurricanes had already devastated Florida as well as numerous tornadoes.We got there two days before hurricane Ivan, unpacked and then had to evacuate to a small town in Alabama. Tornado warnings went off and we took refuge in the hotel room, praying and believing in God for our safety. God again miraculously provided safety and shelter during that devastating storm. He gave us real-life adventure, difficulty and adversity to teach us that HE is our refuge, and He proved it to us time and time again.

As we traveled from California to Florida we had asked God for a sign to confirm that we were on the right path. Very soon afterward, we looked out of the car window and saw a large billboard with the words, "God still fulfills promises," and the scripture in Psalm 46:1. We read it from the Bible and it says, "God is our refuge and strength, an ever present help in time of trouble." We were reassured but didn't give it much thought at the time. That night, however, there was no doubt. A storm was approaching and it was getting late, so we took an unexpected turn into a town that wasn't on our predetermined map course. We arrived in Fort Stockton, Texas and finally settled into the third hotel we came to. What a blessing that place was! The hotel atmosphere was peaceful and relaxing. It *felt* like God was there! When we entered our hotel room, Laura noticed that the Bible displayed on the nightstand was opened to Psalm 46. We knew that had to be more than coincidence. God was truly bringing us into a place of refuge and healing. The inside of the hotel was beautifully decorated like an indoor tropical garden and had an indoor jacuzzi. Laura had been wishing she could go in a jacuzzi, and the water had been turned off for a while so it wasn't too hot to be unsafe for the baby. That might not be a big deal for someone else, but when you have a very pregnant wife traveling across the country who was tired and anxious about arriving safely, that was a wonderful blessing from the Lord. She never even mentioned it out loud, but the Lord knew and He blessed her. He was saying, "Relax, I've got everything covered. You're safe with me."

One night two months before leaving to go to Florida, I was awakened by the word "Succoth." Succoth was the first location where the Israelites camped on their exodus. The word is translated as booth or shelter. It was the first experience for Israel to rest and sleep, not in buildings centered in cities surrounded by conveniences and security, but in the desert. They were vulnerable to the elements, wild animals and hostile nations. Later on in the harvest feast they were to commemorate this lifestyle in an outdoor shelter for seven days and rejoice at the harvest (Leviticus 23:42). God chose the remembrance at the Feast of Tabernacles to teach the Israelites to be thankful and remind them that He was their source of provision and protection. They were to seek Him for refuge. Psalms 91:4 says, "He will cover you with His feathers and under His wings you will find refuge. His faithfulness will be your shield and rampart." God brought us from San Diego and moved us two thousand miles into the path of one of the worst hurricanes to hit Pensacola in one hundred years. He brought us out by faith to trust in His divine protection against every hostile element and adversity the enemy set before us.

Driving out Shame and Humiliation

Another thing God had to heal us from was shame and humiliation. These are enemies of our soul. Shame and humiliation are powerful emotions that can have a significant impact on a person's mental and emotional well-being. Sometimes it comes from our own poor decisions and behavior, and at other times shame and humiliation comes from the harsh words and actions of others. Shame and humiliation can also come from things such as chronic poverty, handicaps and other things beyond our ability to control. These negative emotions can arise from a wide range of experiences, including public embarrassment, personal failure, and social rejection. The effects of shame and humiliation can be far-reaching, impacting a person's self esteem, relationships, and overall quality of life.

One of the most damaging effects of shame and humiliation is the way it can erode a person's self esteem. When a person experiences these negative emotions, they may begin to question their worth and value as a person. This can lead to feelings of inadequacy, self-doubt, and low self-confidence, making it difficult for them to engage with others and pursue their goals. The enemy weaponizes shame and humiliation as an attempt to neutralize the power and effectiveness of Christians so that they are defiled by bitterness, rejection, self-pity and pride, causing them to become unfit for the Master's greater purposes. Sometimes he employs other Christians or even ourselves to do his dirty work. Satan will utilize the words of others as well as ourselves to inflict shame, criticism, false judgments and a sense of rejection, which result in feelings of deep humiliation. It is an excruciating, corrosive emotion. Shame causes people to feel inherently bad, defective and wrong at the core of who they are as a human being.

When we have been deeply hurt, sometimes we begin to entertain negative thoughts that turn our hearts away from God. This comes from the accuser and our adversary, but it is another test we must overcome. We must resist the temptation to feel disappointed with God, but the other test of our heart is whether or not we take up the role of an intercessor. Intercessors are to pray for those the enemy used to perpetuate injustice and inflict emotional pain.

We must learn to recognize the temptation of the enemy to exploit pain, shame, humiliation and disgrace, and turn our heart away from God, because these painful emotions will turn into further discouragement, anger and resentment. These negative emotions feed fear, anxiety and worry, but they are also intended to cause us to break faith with God. We must learn to drive those voices out by lifting our Shield of Faith and wielding the Sword of the Spirit. The word of God and the power of Jesus's blood are anointed to break the power of the enemy, but we must choose to believe in the weapons God has given us.

Fortunately, there is hope for those who struggle with shame and humiliation. Jesus Christ offers a message of hope and healing for all who are burdened by these negative emotions. Through His teaching and example, Jesus shows us that we are beloved children of God, worthy of love and acceptance. There are many examples in scripture where God's children cried out for God to take away the reproach and fear of being humiliated at the hands of their enemies. Note one such plea from Psalm 2:1.. "Do not let me be put to shame, nor let my enemies triumph over me. No one whose hope is in you will ever be put to shame, but they will be put to shame who are treacherous without excuse. Guide me in your truth and teach me, for You are God my Savior, and my hope is in You all day long."

One of the most powerful ways Jesus sets us free is through His unconditional love. Jesus teaches us that we are loved not because of what we do, but simply because we are God's children. This love can help us overcome feelings of shame, rejection, humiliation or fear of embarrassment, as we learn to see ourselves as deeply valued by our Father and worthy of love. He loves us because the Spirit of His Son lives in us.

Another way Jesus sets us free is through His forgiveness. When we make mistakes or experience some sort of failure, it can be easy to feel embarrassed or perhaps even humiliated. However, Jesus offers us forgiveness, reminding us that we are all imperfect and in need of grace. We all fall short of the glory of God. This forgiveness can help us let go of our negative emotions and move forward in help and confidence.

Jesus paid the price for our fears, our sin, and all the pain that has been inflicted upon us through His death and resurrection. God doesn't remember all our past failures or the shame associated with those things, and He doesn't want us to remember that pain, either. "As far as the east is from the west, so far has He removed our transgressions from us." Psalm 103:12. It is comforting to know that God has chosen to forget our past. God Most High is the final authority and He has chosen to extend grace. None of us deserve it, but it's not about whether or not we deserve anything. It's about His desire to show mercy and His great love towards us. To everyone that chooses to believe in the Son of God, He gives the right to become His children. In Isaiah 43:18-20 He says, "Forget the former things; do not dwell on the past. See! I am doing a new thing! Now it springs up. Do you not perceive it?" God calls us to forget the things that are behind us and focus forward on running the race. We cannot run well if we are always looking behind us. Let God take care of the past!

God has promised that those that put their trust in Him would not be put to shame. It takes a focused effort to rehearse His promises and let His good intentions towards us cause all the painful words of others to pale in comparison. If you have agreed with the many voices of accusation, self condemnation, shame, humiliation, reproach, self rejection and inferiority, it's time to be intentional and speak it out loud that you are canceling that agreement (and the assignment of the enemy that he has been enforcing against you!).

The key to overcoming is through humility, which is not at all the same as being humiliated. When we humble ourselves before God, it is to accept His truth and what He has said about us rather than elevating the hurtful words and criticisms of others above His word. Humility also doesn't try to put a proud spin on our failures or shift the blame onto others. It takes responsibility for our faults, is honest about them, and then puts our trust in God to restore rather than looking to man. We never have to gain the approval of a rival or someone that has been instrumental in wounding us in order for God to do something miraculous. God's intentions towards us are always healing, reconciliation and restoration, but He does resist us when we are acting proud. We are reminded to first submit to God (repentance and confession), then we can resist the enemy and he must leave.

We overcome all the enemy's tactics through the blood of Jesus and the word of our testimony. Shame needs secrecy and our agreement in order to remain a negative oppressive force in our life. But, when we tell our story honestly and in humility, the anointing comes upon us for breakthrough and healing others. The enemy has no power over us as we share our testimonies because telling our stories is what breaks the fear of rejection and embarrassment the enemy holds against us. God has promised that His children will not be put to shame if we put our confidence in Him. "Instead of shame and dishonor, you will enjoy a double share of honor. You will possess a double portion of prosperity in your land, and everlasting joy will be yours," (Isaiah 61:7).

The negative effects of shame and humiliation can be significant, impacting a person's self-esteem, relationships and overall quality of life. However, through the beautiful example of Jesus' sacrificial life, His teachings and His forgiveness, we can find healing and hope. By embracing His message of love and forgiveness, we can overcome our negative emotions and live a life of joy and purpose.

Living by faith is a walk that makes a person open to failure, attack and persecution. It is also the most invigorating, challenging, adventurous and exciting way God chooses to live out His dream. Many times, we have felt that God was not in front of us anymore. We had to be reminded that He who goes ahead of us to prepare the way is also the one who goes behind us to stand between the past and the present. When Joshua and the children of Israel were to cross the Jordan river, the priest carrying the Ark of the Covenant stepped into the water and the river parted. The river piled up in a heap from the town called Adam. The river was completely cut off. When Christ died and shed his blood, the river of shame, sin, and guilt that flowed down from the first Adam was completely cut off by the high priest of our confession, Jesus. We have been given access to our Promised Land because He has made the way.

When you're in transition, life can get very uncomfortable. You learn to trust God for income, health, connections, and a variety of other things. It becomes especially burdensome when your wife is expecting a baby. Three days after Hurricane Ivan, we started making our way back to Florida. We had evacuated 300 miles Northeast to a small town called Opelika, Alabama. It had been the only hotel available within a relatively short distance. Our first attempt going back was to drive as far as a tank of gas could go and safely return if the road became impassable. As we came to that point of no return, we started to pray about whether we should go any further. There were cars lined up at every gas station, but there was no electricity to operate the pumps. Restrooms, power, water and ATMs were hit and miss throughout the Panhandle and Southern Alabama. Many roads were closed and I needed to make a decision. Would we turn back to Montgomery for another night in a hotel or continue towards home? We prayed and decided to go back and try again the next day. Again, as we approached that point of no return, my heart raced inside of me. I had a pregnant wife, two cats and a dog counting on me to get them home safely. All I could think of was being stranded on a deserted road with no gas and temperatures of 95°. There is a point of no return for all who walk by faith. It's when God has powerfully worked in your life and has drawn you out. He may burn all your bridges. There's no going back and you can only go forward. As I pressed on, I held my wife's hand and we prayed. The Lord led us safely all the way home. We dodged down trees, power lines, and debris, but we did have a path made perfect only by the father.

Observing all the damage and debris on such a large scale was overwhelming. Thousands of acres of trees were damaged or completely blown over by the 180 mile an hour winds. Homes and buildings throughout Northern Florida and Southern Alabama were either destroyed or received substantial damage. The apartments that we were living in received very little damage and no flooding. We were very thankful. One local resident had commented weeks later that the hurricane, although it had caused considerable damage, had removed old growth. Trees that had been diseased and were a breeding ground for worm and bark eating insects were now going to be separated from the good growth. When transplanting a root bound plant, the dead branches and foliage are usually pruned and discarded. Jesus uses storms and many other trials of life to prune away unbelief and the things that will be dead weight. He will take his pruning shears to our attitudes, activities, relationships, and our motives, among other things. He will prune everything that will inhibit his vine from producing quality fruit for the Kingdom of God.

Israel was put to the test in the wilderness. Pharaoh's Army and chariots were doing the backstroke under the Red Sea, but they weren't out of trouble yet. The Amalekites were waiting for them (Exodus 17:8). Amalekites were big trouble all right. These were people of tall stature and very intimidating to the Israelites. There comes a time when we all have to face our giants. Sometimes it's our fears or a character flaw within ourselves. Sometimes it's another person or relationship that must be dealt with. We can't always take others with us into the Promised Land, and God knows the reasons why. He won't let you take dead weight into your future. It will always slow you down or possibly even disqualify you from certain areas of fruitfulness and ministry. You know who and what those giants are. They stand in bold opposition to you being able to move forward. We will always encounter some giants on the road that leads to our land of promise and dreams fulfilled. The enemy isn't going to let you take ground away from him without a battle. You'll probably incur some battle wounds, but that's just all the more reason to put your faith in the one who is commander of the army of hosts.

God desired to have his children know him not only as The Great I Am, but also as Jehovah Rapha and Jehovah Nissi. He is the Lord that heals and He is our victor. In Exodus 15:25 the Lord tested His people when they came to a place called Marah. The thirsty Israelies were tired and weary, having traveled in the desert. They were looking for water but found the water was bitter and undrinkable. He said, "If you listen carefully to the voice of the Lord your God and do what is right in His eyes, if you pay attention to His commands and keep all His decrees, I will not bring on you any of the diseases I brought on the Egyptians, for I am the Lord who heals you." As I was working on clearing some trees from the hurricane, I accidentally came upon some poison oak. It began to spread and cover 75% of my body. The pain became unbearable and I went to the emergency room but they didn't do anything for my pain relief. For 3 weeks I cried out to the Lord for healing. I would walk the floors crying out to God. I was in too much agony to sleep. Between my fatigue and constant pain, I began to grow weary in my prayers. My wife lifted me up and nursed me back to health. I tried every home remedy I could find but nothing brought much comfort. It was a relief when it finally left my body. Two weeks after that, I had a scratch that was infected in the lymph node under my arm swelled to the size of a grapefruit. More physical ailments kept us close to the Lord in prayer. During this time, my wife's pregnancy had multiple challenges, she was in constant pain, and we felt the vulnerability of our situation. The enemy brought discouragement, anger, and worry. When you're going through difficulty, it is so important to not complain and allow anger or resentment to grab hold of your heart, because it will come out of your mouth. Laura and I have had to deal with the negative, hurtful words of others that made us feel shamed, humiliated, and belittled. Those negative words undermined our ability to see ourselves the way God saw us, and we unknowingly came into agreement with the enemy that was prophesying our future. The adversary used the voices of people that despised us to tell us that our future was hopeless, we would never be successful, and our reputations were destroyed beyond hope. The enemy used the physical pain and emotional stress of what we were going through along with the voices of other people's negativity, threats, word curses, and the rejection we felt, to try to convince us that we were cursed and that God had abandoned us. The enemy wanted us to feel as though he had won and we were totally defeated. Those were some of the lies that we had to take captive and put under submission to God. What we both underestimated was the length of time it took to receive the revelation where we had unknowingly come into agreement with the accuser and believed those lies. It creates a silent partnership in the spirit realm that allows the enemy to enforce those agreements.

When we're going through trials the enemy works overtime to turn our heart away from God. If Satan can get us to change our confession and agree with him, or if he can get us to slander or accuse God and others because of the hurt that was caused, then he can change the course of our destiny and keep us stuck. Satan wants us to be bitter. He wants us to be as full of poison as possible. If we remain that way, we'll remain broken vessels, unable to be used for God's greater purposes. It's Satan who always wants to make us feel as though God isn't trustworthy, but that is the farthest thing from the truth. That is why it takes real humility and a willingness to pray and ask God to reveal what hinders our ability to prosper and be in health. God wants to help us understand where we have made ungodly covenants with a spirit of unbelief because those are areas where we have rejected His truth. We cannot prosper when we have agreed with the enemy that we will be unsuccessful, or failed to believe that God has a better future for us. The enemy uses those areas of unbelief to cause us to feel discouraged, agitated and discontent, knowing it produces striving. God wants us to cease striving and come to a place of rest where our trust is wholly in Him. We have to recognize where an ungodly spirit has been the driving force behind our efforts. What motivates you to do the things you do? Sometimes we fool ourselves into believing we have noble purposes when we are actually driven by a negative belief about ourselves. Who are you trying to prove yourself to? Sometimes we need to recognize when we have been trying to prove to ourselves that the enemy wasn't right about us. When you're trying to prove that the enemy wasn't right in his assessment, you've agreed with his declaration over your life. It puts you in covenant with a spirit of poverty, because poverty is a mindset, not just something that affects your finances. The fact that there is a spirit of agreement between you and spirits of darkness works as a self fulfilling prophecy, and that needs to be broken with a declaration of renouncement. Break that ungodly covenant and put the blood of Jesus over it! The *enemy* is the accuser of the brethren. The liar and accuser is the one who will utilize any mouth that yields to him, including your own! The destroyer is the one who screams the word defeated in your ears. The adversary wants to steal your vision and make you feel that your failures are too big for God to fix. The father of lies tells you there's no redemption for your future. If you're hearing those accusations in your head or from others, don't trust those voices. It's not the voice of your heavenly Father!

During times when your faith is under attack, you must encourage yourself in the Lord. We knew that God had brought us to Florida. We remembered his kindness and graciousness as he spoke to us, reminding us of his love and faithfulness. We remembered how he brought us through the deserts of Arizona and New Mexico during a heat wave. I towed a $2,500 lb trailer with a 4-cylinder Nissan. I was afraid the car would overheat and break down in the desert, but God brought us through safely. God spared us from the disaster of a hurricane, and not one item was damaged or destroyed. He protected us and provided for us time and time again. He didn't bring us out to have us die in the wilderness. The Psalmist cried out in Psalm 42:5-6, "Why are you downcast, oh my soul? Why are you so disturbed within me? Put your hope in God, for I will yet praise Him, My Savior and my God. My soul is downcast within me; therefore, I will remember you from the land of Jordan, the heights of Herman in Mount Mizar." David cried out as he was in flight from the enemy's attempts to destroy him. He put his hope in God. He prayed to his God and Savior. David acknowledged that God was there. Men may ask you in mockery, "Where is your God?" They think in their hearts, let Him save you. But, like David who knew God was present, we put our hope in God. In Psalm 139:7-8 it says, "Where can I go from your Spirit? Where can I flee from your presence? If I rise on the wings of the dawn, if I settle on the far side of the sea, even there your hand will guide me. Your right hand will hold me fast." God has big hands. He won't drop you!

The reality of our situations can be in conflict with the presence of faith. In Luke 18:8, Jesus asked an important, probing question of his disciples. He asked if he would really find faith on the earth when he returned. This was a summary question to a parable describing a woman's injustice from her adversary. The woman had no family to plead her cause and she could not afford an attorney to represent her. All she had was a great need and tenacity, a hunger to see her injustice overturned. We have a just judge in our heavenly Father. We have an advocate that will go to the Father on our behalf and His name is Jesus. We have a key witness in the Spirit who will testify to the legal petition presented before heaven's court. The only thing the Lord requires from us is persistent faith. The conversation between your soul and spirit during times of conflict can be very intense. In Psalm 42:11, it's faith that gets the final word. "Put your hope in God, for I will yet Praise him, My Savior and my God." Faith declares what our Spirit man knows is the truth, and faith has the last word.

Driving out Insecurity, Doubt and Mediocrity

The Dream Giver, a fictional book by Bruce Wilkinson, shares the challenges of Ordinary as he traveled into the Valley of the Giants. He steps into the valley but realizes that he is not ready to face a giant. He needs more training and preparation. Ordinary heard footsteps that had him hiding in a bush. He didn't know at first that the noise was actually the Commander who had come to encourage him."Hail, brave warrior!" the Being called out. "I'm no warrior, mumbled Ordinary. "I'm a Nobody from the Land of Familiar." "Every nobody who comes this far is a warrior," said the Being. "Don't be afraid of any giant, Ordinary," said the Commander. "They're real. They're enormous. They block the path of your Dream. But if you believe in the Dream Giver and you're willing to take a Big Risk, you will get past them." "But I have no weapons or armor!" exclaimed Ordinary. Then the Commander helped Ordinary to see how the Dream Giver had been preparing him for battle since the day he left Familiar. "Beware of Unbelief, Ordinary," said the Commander. "Unbelief is much more dangerous to your Dream than any giant!" And then the Commander was gone.(Wilkinson, Multnomah Books, 2003).

The Dream Giver is a story about a hero named Ordinary, but let's take a look at some real life Bible heroes. David sings out in Psalm 144:1, "Praise be to the Lord my rock who trains my hands for war, my fingers for battle." David was the shepherd boy who later became king. In his youth, he killed the bear and the lion, not knowing the training of faith and loyalty that would catapult him to one of the most famous duels in the Bible, the battle with a giant named Goliath. Warriors are trained to not only learn to fight their own battles, but they help others fight their battles.

From day one, the Lord uses the events in our lives to prepare us for battles with the enemy or a divine appointment with the king. In the book of Esther, we learn of a young orphan girl who was chosen by the sovereign will of God to be queen. The story goes into great detail about the lengthy preparation Esther received in anticipation for one night with the king. At the time, Esther did not realize how significant it was, because God had not revealed His greater purposes; but, God was positioning her for a future opportunity to find favor with the king in order to plead the cause of her fellow Jews, who had been targeted for destruction. God's bigger plan was for Esther to save a nation, but it would require great trust, great faith, and great humility. Esther found favor with the king because she set her heart on understanding what the king preferred. She sought to find ways that would please him. Esther set her heart and soul to be ready to receive a life altering opportunity, to spend one memorable night with the king. This is all together unusual as orphan girls are usually not of the caliber suitable for a king. Women of pedigree, acceptable social class, and a rich inheritance would have been preferred, but God intervened. Esther did in fact become queen, but more importantly, she won the heart of her king. The new queen was about to learn a kingdom lesson. Favor is never given to promote selfishness. Favor is given in order to be a blessing to others. Queen Esther was forced to reveal her true identity, a place of no turning back, in order to seek favor with the king on behalf of her people. God raised her up for the precise time in history to be a deliverer to her people.

Let's take a closer look at some of the characters that have been mentioned. Ordinary was ready to face the giants; not on his own merit, but on his faith in the Dream Giver that had led him to this point. Esther faced the giant in her life that wanted to destroy her and her people. David faced numerous battles and the current reigning King Saul, who tried to destroy him. What is your giant? Is there something or someone that is poised as an enemy of the dream God has given you? If that enemy is using unfair, unethical or ungodly methods to destroy you, hinder your ability to move forward, or stand in opposition to prevent you from claiming your promises, then rest assured it is the Lord's battle and he will help you fight it.

35

ROOM TO GROW

We do not fight with the tactics like the rest of the world. It is God that presents opportunities at the right time. He's able to open doors through his favor and grace, and get us around the obstacles. His favor towards us can open doors that would not be open to us any other way, even if we lack the necessary credentials for the position. His favor does for us what we cannot do for ourselves. God gives us his methods as our weapons, and he gives us our Promised Land as a gift of His grace. It is God that chooses our inheritance. "The Lord is the portion of my inheritance and my cup. You support my lot. The lines have fallen to me in pleasant places, indeed my heritage is beautiful to me." (Psalm 16:5-6).

The battles that stand between us and our Promised Land will be won through faith in the King of Kings. The Commander of the Army of Hosts, the Rider on the White Horse, Jesus Christ, will defeat them as we exercise our faith. When God leads us to those appointed times in our life, he looks to the faith and trust in our heart. He knows our skills and abilities as well as our weaknesses. In second Samuel 5:23, David once again met the enemy in the Valley of the Giants. David inquired of the Lord and the Lord said to David,"As soon as you hear the sound of marching in the tops of the balsam trees, move quickly, because that will mean the Lord has gone out in front of you to strike the Philistine army." God instructs David to circle around the Philistines and attack them from behind, rather than engaging them head-on. This strategy proved successful, and David was able to defeat the Philistines. The significance of this event lies in the fact that David recognized the importance of seeking God's guidance in his decision-making. He understood that his strength and success came not from his own abilities, but from God's guidance and direction. By listening and following God's instructions, David was able to achieve victory over his enemies.

Insecurity, doubt and mediocrity brought Israel a 40-year detour when the opportunity to take their Promised Land presented itself. In Numbers 13:31-32, ten of the twelve spies that went to spy out the land came back and reported a different story than Joshua and Caleb. They also said that they saw giants in the land, and that they themselves felt like grasshoppers in comparison. This report caused the people to rebel against Moses and Aaron, and even to suggest that they should choose a new leader and return to Egypt (Numbers 14:1-4).

Faith was killed by the bad report of the ten spies. The negativity of unbelief spread discouragement among the Israelites about the land they had explored. This caused the people to feel overwhelmed and defeated before they ever went to battle, and the people refused to extend their faith. God had already proven He was with them by showing numerous signs, wonders and miracles, and He expected the Israelites to trust Him to be with them for the conquest of the land. After the people had rebelled and refused to trust God's promise to give them the land, God declared that they would wander in the wilderness for forty years until the entire generation who had rebelled had died. When the people heard this, they became sorrowful and decided to take matters into their own hands. They presumed that if they went up to the land of Canaan, they would be able to conquer it, even though God had said that he would not go with them (Numbers 14:41-43). God determined that they would not inherit their Promised Land. They forfeited the opportunity to move with purpose. They wandered aimlessly in the wilderness enduring trial after trial, one year for each of the 40 days of the spies' journey.

When we go through trying times, we must be careful not to bring discouragement to others. Negativity and unbelief can cause ourselves and others to doubt the faithfulness of God. We never know who looks to us as a role model of our faith. God is able to do exceedingly, abundantly more than we could ask or think. Is anything too difficult for the Lord? Even if your mind is telling you negative things, train your mouth to speak words of faith. If you don't, you will put the enemy on assignment to bring those negative words to pass. We must be determined to have the response of faith and speak the right things. As Joshua and Caleb cried out, "Do not rebel against the Lord and do not be afraid of the people of the land, because we will swallow them up. Their protection is gone but the Lord is with us. Do not be afraid of them." (Numbers 14:9).

The Israelites had heard the promises of God. In Exodus 23:27 God said,"I will send my terror ahead of you and throw into confusion every nation you encounter. I will make all your enemies turn their backs and run. I will send the hornet ahead of you to drive out the Hivites, the Canaanites and the Hittites out of your way. In Leviticus 26:8 it also says, "Five of you will chase 100, and 100 of you will chase 10,000, and your enemies will fall by the sword before you." Insecurity and doubt had resulted in the Israelites' disobedience. They went from rebellion in Numbers 13 to presumption in Numbers 14 because they refused to trust God and His promises. They rebelled against Moses and Aaron because they were afraid of the people in Canaan and did not believe that God was able to give them the land. Then, when God said that they would not receive the land, they presumptuously decided to take it anyway, even though God had said that he would not be with them. In both cases, the Israelites failed to trust God and his promises, and instead relied on their own understanding and abilities.

A lack of faith, replaced with presumption, eventually led them to take steps to go to battle, but the Lord was no longer with them. The account of the story is found in Numbers 14:44. The Israelites felt badly for their sins, but even though they acknowledge their disobedience, in their hearts true repentance had not taken place. Rebellion was still in their heart. When they told Moses they decided to go to war against the Amalekites, Moses warned them it was too late. Presumption caused them to be driven by their guilt, fear, and pride, and they again disobeyed the council of their leader. They went up against the Amalekites and Canaanites without the ark, which symbolized the presence of God. They went without their leader and suffered a terrible defeat. You would think that they would have been concerned when both God and Moses stayed behind, but the headstrong Israelites went forward with their plans anyway. It is sad to say, but many of us act like that at times, too. The Israelites were warned not to go up to the Promised Land because the Lord was not with them, but they disobeyed and were defeated by the Amalekites and Canaanites. The verse reads, "But they presumed to go up to the heights of the hill country, although neither the ark of the covenant of the Lord nor Moses departed out of the camp." (Numbers 14:44)

In a modern-day setting, this concept might apply to situations where people are warned or advised against taking certain actions, but they choose to ignore the warnings and proceed anyway. The lesson for us is to heed warnings and advice, especially when they come from trusted sources, and not to presume that everything will work out just because we want it to or because we think we know better. Pride and a headstrong attitude often results in wrong decisions that can result in regret, disappointment and self-condemnation when things don't work out as we hoped. Our wrong decisions will affect others, too, and can result in hurt and offense to people that we have involved when it wasn't God leading our decisions. Time in the wilderness is to help us learn how to humble ourselves, listen and follow directions. It is important to carefully consider the potential risks and consequences of our actions before making decisions, and to seek guidance and counsel from those who are more knowledgeable or experienced.

ROOM TO GROW

When we allow our fears, pride, presumption and our needs to drive us, they will drive us into places we do not want to go, and ultimately result in defeat. God does not break His promises. He is an ever-present help in times of trouble. However, He does not want us to act out of impatience just because we feel we need to be doing something. It is presumptuous to think we can do what sounds good to us and assume God blesses our plans when He has not spoken. The presumption of pride and immaturity is to proceed with our own plans when we do not have clarity of exactly what God is saying, or the timing of when to act. God knows the intents of our heart better than we do because He knows what motivates us. Pride and presumption led the Israelites into rebellion and their defeat. Somewhere on the road of faith they had thrown away their confidence, then they allowed a sense of guilt to drive their behavior. Let us not make the same mistakes. Faith, clarity and obedience should motivate our actions. Hebrews 10:35 states,"Don't throw away your confidence, it will be richly rewarded." These stories highlight the importance of seeking God's guidance and direction in our own lives. It reminds us that we are not meant to go through life on our own, but rather to rely on God's wisdom and guidance. If we are willing to listen to God and follow His instructions, He will help us learn to overcome obstacles and achieve success in our endeavors.

A time of transition is a time of preparation and learning God's ways. He isn't worried about giving us all the answers. He gives us experiences instead, and through those experiences, we learn His ways. It is a time of testing, a time rich with opportunities to build our faith. It is a time to enlarge our vision as we see the God of our impossibilities help us conquer those giants that come against our faith. It is a time of healing and restoration, and a time when we have our strength renewed like the eagles. He reassures us of His presence as well as coming into the understanding of our identity in Christ and how to walk under His authority in our lives. It is a time of refining and refinishing as God puts the polish on the new vessels we have become. It is a time of reveling in His presence, hearing His voice, and falling deeper in love with the King of Glory. Yes, there are times when it can seem like an eternity before we see the Land of Promise. How many times we moved over the years, each time thinking we had come into our Promised Land, when in reality it was another stop in the wilderness. It takes time for God to grow us up, but in each stage of our development there are many opportunities for growth, lessons to be learned, new relationships to enjoy and areas to exercise our dominion for the sake of enlarging His kingdom. One of the biggest indicators that you've reached your Promised Land is that there is a knowing that God has called you to a certain city or location. You can feel His heart in that place, and there is a feeling that you've found home. It's been said that God is God of the suddenlies. We have to be prepared to speak faith and place our life down when the opportunity presents itself. We don't know when that will occur because only God sets the times and seasons. Our responsibility is to be awake, alert, and prepared to go to battle at the sound of the trumpet.

ROOM TO GROW

Prayer for Wisdom and Guidance to Silence the Voice of the Enemy

Dear Heavenly Father,

I come before you today with a humble heart, seeking your guidance and wisdom as I navigate through this time in my life. Help me to learn to listen for your instructions and to be obedient to do as you say, even when it may not make sense to me.

Your word tells me to trust in You with all my heart and not to lean on my own understanding. I know that Your ways are higher than mine, and your thoughts are higher than mine. So, I ask that you would give me the faith and strength to trust in You completely, even when I don't understand. Father, guard me and give me self-control so that I do not enter into rebellion or presumption. Help me not to be impatient with Your timing. Above all, please help me so that I do not make poor decisions and bring hurt or offense to others. I choose to submit myself to the authority of Your Holy Spirit and I ask You for wisdom that will outwit the enemy. Let grace and mercy be ornaments around my neck. Let Your wisdom and discretion preserve me. I ask that I would find favor with You and others, and that my path in life is blessed and prosperous. Help me to be still and quiet before you, so that I can hear your voice above all the noise and distractions of this world. Help me to silence the voice of the enemy by rehearsing Your promises, and refusing to let the voices of fear, shame, and intimidation become influences in my life. Help me drive out the enemy. Give me the discernment to recognize your voice when You give me counsel through the words of others, and the courage to follow your lead, even when it may take me out of my comfort zone.

I pray that I always remember that You are the source of all wisdom and knowledge, and I never forget to give you all the glory and praise. In Jesus' name, amen.

ROOM TO GROW

CHAPTER THREE
THE PURSUIT OF GOD'S PRESENCE

"YOU TRANSPLANTED A VINE OUT OF EGYPT; YOU DROVE OUT THE NATIONS **AND PLANTED IT.** YOU CLEARED THE GROUND FOR IT, AND IT TOOK ROOT AND FILLED THE LAND." PSALM 80:8,9

It is very clear in Scripture that God is the Master Planter and when he tends and oversees His garden, He does it with great thought and planning. Our father knows the exact location for the planting and the soil condition. He knows whether or not the soil is fertile or needs nutrients added to make it rich. He knows the timing of the seasons and the weather conditions of the environment. His garden will always yield the best of crops. He never plants an inferior vine. His Son, Jesus, was chosen before the foundation of the world to be that vine. In John 15:1 the scripture reads, "I am the true vine and my father is the gardener." The father planted Jesus and His kingdom in an open field, which is the world. David stated this in Psalm 31:8 when he said, "You have not handed us over to the enemy, but have set our feet in a spacious place." David was saying that God had not surrendered him or shut him up in the hand of the enemy, but he made David stand in a place where there was a lot of room, a spacious place where he had room to grow. There is unlimited potential for growth in an open field, but we cannot grow or bear fruit unless we abide in God and have a relationship with His Holy Spirit. The things that hinder our growth are the limits we place on God.

Our perception of ourselves and our perception of God are inextricably linked to the depth of relationship we have with the Holy Spirit. Our concept of God can be limited to what others have taught us about him, how we see God move through various churches and ministries, the doctrine of particular denominations, or what we have experienced of Him in our own personal lives. We draw certain conclusions based on whether or not we feel that God has been good to us. When those conclusions are incorrect, then our understanding of Him is equally incorrect. Truth as we understand it is relative only to the degree that we truly know God. That truth also has the capacity to affect how we see ourselves and others. If we do not have a deep, abiding relationship with the Holy Spirit, we will have an extremely limited, misguided perception of our understanding of him. When we cultivate a deep and intimate relationship with the Holy Spirit, we are able to see ourselves and God in a whole new light.

When we are in close relationship with the Holy Spirit, we are able to perceive God's character and nature more clearly. As Jesus said in John 16:13, "When he, the Spirit of truth, comes, He will guide you into all the truth." This guidance from the Holy Spirit helps us to see God as loving, just, merciful, and faithful.

However, when we neglect our relationship with the Holy Spirit, our perception of ourselves and God can become distorted. We may see ourselves as unworthy or unlovable, and we may view God as distant or uncaring. The Holy Spirit is a person, and we must have a deeply personal relationship with Him if we are to know God and have a better understanding of ourselves.

Therefore, it is imperative that we prioritize our relationship with the Holy Spirit if we want to have a healthy perception of ourselves and God. As we draw near to the Holy Spirit in prayer, worship, and study of God's Word, we will be transformed and renewed in our minds. We will see ourselves as God sees us, and we will perceive God's character and nature more clearly.

God is big! There is no end to his power, abilities or His resources. It saddens him when we have such a small perception of Him. It's only our lack of faith that places limits on all the wonderful things He wants to do in us, through us and for us. Enlarge your vision and understanding of Him, because he has great plans for you. He thinks way beyond what we can comprehend. He has big dreams and He thinks, plans, orchestrates, creates, and sees everything in regards to an eternal kingdom. He looks down on the corridor of time and knows how every detail of our lives will be lived out, how every decision we make will affect our future, and the impact we will have on others. He knows exactly what each one of the billions of people on Earth need at any given moment, where we are, what we are doing, what we are saying, what we are thinking, and He knows the number of hairs on each one of our heads. He knows everything! If that doesn't boggle your mind, nothing will! But, how comforting it is to know that he has written a plan for our life with all of these details in mind. Our God is the God of wonders, and He does not consider limits because everything about Him is unable to be contained. His power, resources, and creativity are unmatched and inexhaustible. God doesn't think small and He doesn't plant his vine in a small pot. He plants it in an open field of His kingdom.

Rick Joyner defines the church and the kingdom relationship in his book, ***Delivered from Evil***. Mr. Joyner writes, "The church is not the kingdom, though it is certainly a part of it, and will be the primary vehicle through which the kingdom comes. Even so, His kingdom is far bigger than the church, and the church needs to be His instrument through which He does His work on the earth."(Joyner, Destiny Image, 2004). The problem with many people's thinking is that their concept of the church is limited to what they see around them in their local church. A limited mindset like this can breed jealousy, competition and contention. A kingdom mindset understands there is no need to feel competitive or jealous of others. He's already prepared our inheritance and it has our name on it. It doesn't belong to anyone else. God has called us to be planted in the kingdom. The church exists within every person in whom Christ inhabits. There are many included in the body of Christ that do not attend a local church. There are those that feel they are outcasts or unaccepted by the church at large. There are multitudes that don't fit. Would we believe that God would exclude them from His eternal plan to build the kingdom? Certainly not! Do you think He has a plan to include them in the greater works of kingdom expansion? Absolutely!

In Matthew 13, we find the teachings of the kingdom parables. Jesus defined the parable of the weeds to his disciples. The one who sowed good seeds was the Son of Man. The field was the world. The good seed stands as the sons of the kingdom, while the evil one sowed the weeds. The great harvest will come at the end of the age and the weeds (everything that causes sin in all who do evil) will be pulled up by His angels and cast into the fire. The

42

righteous will shine as the sun in the kingdom of their father, because we will become like his Son.

I found myself as a pastor for many years thinking I was to plant people in the church. Although that sounds predictable and scriptural it was not always spiritual. Romans 14:17 tells us, "The Kingdom of God is not meat or drink but righteousness, peace and joy in the Holy Spirit." The Holy Spirit is at work planting people in God's kingdom and I was planting people in my church. It became my own personal kingdom. I felt the stress of competitiveness within the network of churches and other pastors I was associated with, and fought to overcome the feelings of failure, as I evaluated my ministry. It became an overwhelming burden that shaped my attitudes and expectations of others out of fear of failure. I wanted people to find a place of service in my church so they could help me out with all that I was trying to do for God. Although it was not my intention, I was placing the burdens on the people rather than allowing them to grow and find their place of anointed service where they could use their spiritual gifts. More importantly, I wanted people tithing because I could not advance my agenda without the finances to keep the church operating. This is a snare that many ministry leaders fall into where the message on finances and giving becomes a root of control and manipulation. Although I deeply cared about my congregation, my personal goals got in the way of God's dream and His objective for His kingdom. I had a 'this-is-my-pot' mentality and I wanted people to be planted in my pot.

Before God transplants you into His Promised Land, He transforms your thinking so that you'll be effective and productive in his field. He planted my faith in a king and a kingdom that is bigger than my goals, talents, skills or gifting. Every believer, when they receive Jesus Christ as their Savior, is translated from one kingdom to another immediately. For he has rescued us from the domain of darkness and transferred us into the kingdom of His beloved Son.." (Colossians 1:13).

The transformation comes as we are renewed in our spirits, in the renewal of our minds, and by faith we can be approved in God's perfect will. Paul writes in Philippians 3:7-9, "...but whatever were gains to me I now consider loss for the sake of Christ. What is more, I consider everything a loss because of the surpassing worth of knowing Christ Jesus my Lord, for whose sake I have lost all things. I consider them garbage, that I may gain Christ and be found in Him, not having a righteousness of my own that comes from the law, but that which is through faith in Christ- the righteousness that comes from God on the basis of faith." Self-righteousness, which is a religious spirit, self-promotion, and pleasing people are all part of a root-bound mentality. The Lord prunes or cuts off these attitudes and faulty beliefs so that the fruit we produce is healthy and has eternal value. His desire is for the kingdom's message to be preached with purity, power and authority, not compromised with our own personal agenda.

The intent of wilderness experiences is to deliver us from those things that are weaknesses in our character and those things that have no eternal value in God's kingdom. The wilderness experiences are also there to prepare us for warfare and strengthen our faith. This was emphasized by Moses when he confronted two tribes in Numbers 32:1-32. They wanted to settle their families in Gilead, which was located before the Jordan crossing. Moses was concerned that they were going to shirk their responsibility to their brethren instead of helping them to conquer the territory west of the Jordan River. He was afraid they were going to drop out of the battle before it even took place. Moses rebukes them in verse 7: "Why do you discourage the Israelites from going over to the land that the Lord has given them?" He likened them to their fathers, who at Kadesh Barnea discouraged the Israelites from possessing their

Promised Land. God dealt with them because they did not follow the Lord wholeheartedly. The Lord declared that only Joshua and Caleb were to go into the Promised Land because they were found faithful.

Caleb was commended in Deuteronomy 1:36 for being full of faith and wholehearted obedience towards the Lord. Caleb pleaded the cause for his inheritance in Joshua 14:7-9. "I brought him back a report according to my convictions. I reported what was in my heart, but my brothers who went with me made the hearts of the people melt with fear. I, however, followed the Lord my God wholeheartedly."(KJV). The word 'wholly' comes from the Hebrew word 'mala.' (Strong's Concordance #4390). It is translated as fullness or to be filled. Webster's Dictionary defines it as 'total, sound, intact, complete, unimpaired, healed, uncut, undivided, unbroken and undamaged.'

In Matthew 12:34 Jesus said, "Out of the abundance of the heart the mouth speaks." What your heart is full of will come out at the set time of testing. Whether we realize it or not, we meditate upon the things that are in our heart, and they will eventually come out of our mouths. Those emotions stem from spiritually rooted issues and demonic attachments. Emotions in themselves are not always from bad spirits, but if we listen to the wrong thoughts long enough, the enemy will use those things to gain our agreement so that evil spirits can form assignments against us. For example, if a person repeatedly meditates on things that make them feel angry, they give themselves over to acting out in anger, and they make room for a spirit to attach itself to their life. If we feel rejected, dishonored or disrespected, the thing we focus on is how we will treat others. Blame shifting, unfair fighting, belittling or shaming others are all manipulative forms of verbal abuse that can result when we have unhealed emotional wounds and demonic attachments. If we have been shamed or devalued by people that treated us wrong, we can begin to inflict others out of the same spirit. You know a spirit by the fruit it produces. Those spirits fully intend to trip people up and they will cause character weaknesses to be revealed. When pressure situations arise, what a person has been hiding in their heart will be exposed for all to see.

Satan presents each of us with opportune moments to either bless or speak a curse. A person that cannot speak well of others or looks for opportunities to be critical is not thinking or acting with a renewed mind. Using one's mouth to speak negatively about others is speaking word curses. While the world might not care, God does. Psalm 109: 17 contains a vital truth. Those careless, critical words that are pronounced upon others act as word curses that will find their way back to those that speak them. When words are used to hurt, defile and inflict others, it will strip the anointing and favor off a person's life and ministry. When people cannot bring themselves to celebrate the successes of others or speak blessing, the blessings they desire for themselves are ultimately withheld. It is also important to understand that how a person speaks about others directly reveals what they think about God and His creation, because we are made in His image. A person's love for others or lack of it, is directly proportional to their love for God. When we understand that Father is full of faith and love towards us it brings comfort. No matter how many times we mess up, His heart will always be full of love for His creation because that is who He is. Love is inherent in His divine nature which compels Him to think well of us not only when we succeed in our obedience, but even when we stumble or fail. He continues to think wonderful things about us because He sees us through the eyes of faith. He loves us because the Spirit of His Son lives within us. Jesus will never speak badly about one of his family members. He will always be in our corner rooting for our success. God knows all our weaknesses, loves us anyway, and envisions us as the finished work of Christ. When we get a revelation of just how loving and kind He is, we learn not to entertain negative thoughts about others or even ourselves. Every contrary, pessimistic opinion we have of ourselves is because of an opposing mindset that is reluctant to believe the truth. Limiting mindsets lead us to believe that somehow we are unworthy, unaccepted, or disqualified from receiving God's best. When we understand that we are positioned in the kingdom as dearly loved children with all the benefits of royalty, it changes how we think about ourselves and others. We can bless them freely without fear that somehow we will be shortchanged in the process.

Caleb and Joshua must have known the truth about God and because it manifested as courageous assurance towards God. That attitude of faith produced joy and confidence in their ability to conquer whatever stood in opposition to their inheritance. Their morale was energized with fearlessness and boldness towards God that exemplified unwavering faith. They saw the Majesty of God, His power and His faithfulness, and they knew in their hearts that God would not fail them. They kept their eyes on Him and His promise before them daily while they feasted in His presence. They spoke words of faith because they were assured of what God had said and done. They meditated on His miracles and testimonies of His faithfulness. When the moment came to declare what they had observed, they did not hesitate to speak words of faith. The spirit welled up inside of them and they proclaimed and prophesied the purpose and power of God. David had the same experience when he spoke to Saul in first Samuel 17:32, "Let no one lose heart on account of this Philistine; your servant will go and fight him." The disciples also spoke boldly in the Book of Acts. They were a people that were filled with the Spirit and continually hungered for more of God.

One of the things I noticed in my former ministry and my personal life was a dryness and ineffectiveness. I felt like I was striving to do the work that I needed to do and it continued to drain me spiritually. Part of the problem is that I had been led to believe that once a person was filled with a baptism of the Holy spirit, they had all they needed. Although I knew according to scripture that God had given us everything we needed for a divine life of righteousness, I equated that to not needing more of the Spirit. Subsequently, I didn't continue to ask for more of Him. I saw zealousness in others, but it was a zeal for either more programs or services, or a zealousness produced from selfish ambition. I needed a hunger that consumed my whole being for the presence of God. I needed to keep my lamp full of oil. *Blessed are those who hunger and thirst for righteousness for they shall be filled.* I also needed to learn the true meaning of the scripture, "Seek first the Kingdom of God and His righteousness and all these things will be added unto you." (Matthew 6:33).

People planted in the kingdom have hungry, seeking, faith-filled hearts. A person's way of thinking and living change radically. They exercise their faith and hunger for more of God's Spirit. Joshua and Caleb had been motivated by a hunger that led them into God's presence. In Exodus 33:11, Moses erected a tent of meeting outside the camp. God would come down and visit with Moses and speak to him face to face as He would speak to a friend. When Moses would leave, Joshua stayed behind in God's presence. I believe Joshua saw the relationship between God and Moses and it inspired him to seek more of God for his own life. We should take that lesson to heart. Perhaps we should all ask ourselves, "Does my life inspire others to draw closer to God?" Joshua became a kingdom man as he hungered after God and sought a deeper relationship with him. The presence of God changes a person. It will gloriously ruin you for anything except the Kingdom of God.

If we will allow it to, the presence of God will transform our thinking to a kingdom mindset. My wife and I pursued God's presence with all our heart. We spent our time running after His presence because we knew the anointing would change us. We looked for meetings in different churches to worship with God's people. Our desire was to present our hearts whenever the opportunity came to respond to an altar call. We would cry out for His touch upon our lives. We filled our apartment with worship and praise and found ourselves waking up in the middle of the night praying and worshiping. We woke up with praise on our lips and went to bed with worship on our hearts. Our conversations throughout the day were filled with revelations of God's mercy and grace, and the different things he was speaking to us through His word and through our dreams. We read books written by Spirit-filled authors that were about the pursuit of His presence, the Holy Spirit, renewal and revival. We became captivated by the Holy Spirit and passionate for His presence. We did everything we knew how to get more of the Lord. During this time, we noticed that the Lord also restricted us from activities, developing new friendships and anything else that was a distraction. He wanted our undivided attention. It became apparent that He wanted to be the sole focus of our attention and our adoration. God's presence is enough because there is such joy in knowing Him.

Pastor Bill Johnson, the author of the book, *When Heaven Invades Earth,* shares his personal Insight on pursuing God. "In our endeavor to pursue His presence in spiritual gifts I must desire life-changing encounters with God, over and over again. I must cry out day and night for them and be specific. I must be willing to travel to get what I need. If God is moving somewhere else more than where I live, I must go! If he is using someone more than He is using me, I must humbly go to them and ask them to pray for me with the laying on of hands. Some may ask, "Why can't God touch me where I am?" He can. But he usually moves in ways that emphasize our need for others, rather than adding to our independence. Wise men have always been willing to travel."(Johnson, Destiny Image, 2005). We have gone to altars time and time again. People may ask, "Don't you weary God with your constant presence at the altar?" I am reminded of a story about a tenacious widow. Jesus encouraged His disciples to be persistent with their continual pleas and petitions. Who will get justice? Who will get the blessing? The hungry. In that same chapter in Luke 18 is the story of blind Bartimaeus who was told to be quiet, but he shouted all the more. That persistence is what caused Jesus to stop and ask what the man wanted Him to do. Genuine faith always meets resistance, and faith will always require something of us. Our tenacity is what grabs God's attention. When Jesus stops to look at you, what will you do? It's as though He's asking, "What are you willing to go through to get your blessing? How many demons are you willing to fight? How many insults are you willing to endure? If I don't answer you right away, will you keep asking or just give up? What are you willing to sacrifice in order to receive the blessing of God?" Jesus asks all of us a question. "Will I really find faith on the Earth and will I find it in you?" The effectual, fervent prayer of a righteous man or woman avails much. It's the pursuit of God with our whole heart. God is continually looking for those He can bless."The eyes of the Lord run to and fro throughout the whole earth, to show himself strong on behalf of those whose heart is perfect towards him."(2 Chronicles 16:9 KJV).

Prayer for Living in the Presence of God

Dear Heavenly Father,

I ask You to bless me with my spiritual language and baptize me in the Holy Spirit. Holy Spirit, I want you. I need you. I am passionate for your Spirit. Create in me a continuous hunger and thirst for Your presence. Come, Holy Spirit, and possess me. Baptize me in fire. Fill me. I need to be clothed with power from on high. Please fill me with rivers of living water that are spoken about in John 7:38, where Jesus said that whoever believes in Him, out of his innermost being would flow rivers of living water. Jesus, I do believe in You. I confess You as the risen Son of the Most High God, who died for my sins and rose again to give me victory over the evil one. Thank You for rivers of living water flowing from within me, and answering my request for more of your Holy Spirit.

Holy Spirit, I also ask that you would renew my mind. Transform my thinking to align with heaven's perspective. Help my natural mind to get out of the way so that I can see every situation from a perspective of faith. I pray for steadfast faith to see miracles come forth. In Jesus name I pray, Amen.

ROOM TO GROW

CHAPTER FOUR
THE PREPARATIONATION PROCESS

"YOU TRANSPLANTED A VINE OUT OF EGYPT; YOU DROVE OUT THE NATIONS AND PLANTED IT.
YOU CLEARED THE GROUND FOR IT, AND IT TOOK ROOT AND FILLED THE LAND." PSALM 80:8,9

Transplanting is a simple term that means lifting and resetting a plant from one place to another. This can apply to people also. The definition is very simple but the process is more complex. When God transplants us from one place to another, He does things at a set time, in a prescribed way, at a specific place. Psalms 80: 9 can also read, "You made a ready place for it," or " You made room for it." Jesus told his disciples in John 14:2, " I am going there to prepare a place for you," and He also told them, "You know the way to the place where I'm going." Jesus makes the place ready and shows us the way at the appointed time. He told his disciples He would come back and take them to be with him. God's patterns for the eternal and spiritual kingdom display His sovereign rule over our lives. The Bible assures us that all things work together for the good of those who love God, who've been called according to His purpose. God has predestined us to be conformed to the likeness of his Son. Those God predestined He also called.

There are many biblical examples to show us that God does in fact raise up certain individuals for specific purposes throughout history. Joseph was raised up for the purpose of being a deliverer to others, including the family that tried to kill his dream and sold him into slavery. At the time when his brothers were plotting against him, neither Joseph nor his family knew where that series of events would lead them. Nevertheless, God had it all planned out ahead of time. Isn't it great that nothing catches God by surprise? In order to accomplish God's purposes, it was necessary for Joseph to be transplanted from his family at Bethel to Pharaoh's courts in Egypt. The events of Joseph's life created a difficult transition for him, but it was for God's divine purpose. Every maneuver on his journey was meant to position Joseph to be in the right place at the right time, but for that to occur, Joseph had to be in jail where he would eventually meet the Pharaoh's cupbearer and baker. Joseph had no idea why he was falsely accused and ended up in prison. Little did he know that as he exercised his spiritual gifts, one of those people he ministered to would eventually be the person that recommended Joseph to Pharaoh when Pharaoh was desperate for someone that could interpret a troublesome dream. The cupbearer was a key individual God used to connect Joseph to his destiny connection that would catapult him into power at just the right time to save his own family, as well as an entire nation from famine. When we can't see God's purpose in the pain or adversity of difficult circumstances, let us remember that He knows how to get us in position for promotion. He knows who to give that dream to, and he knows who to nudge at the right time so that the right person remembers our name.

Another example is the life of Moses. He escaped to the desert after killing an Egyptian and spent many years in exile. He learned how to live as a shepherd and depend on God in the wilderness. Moses was transplanted from leading sheep in the desert to leading a nation into freedom. Moses, the man chosen by God to lead over a million people out of bondage, was born to be a deliverer, but he felt the least qualified to do the job and came up with many excuses. Moses was insecure about his speaking abilities yet called to confront the most powerful ruler of his time to demand that he let the Israelites go free. This only made the Pharaoh mad, so he punished God's people with hard bondage. God called Moses to be His chosen servant, and took His time developing His heart into Moses, so that Moses would understand His ways. In spite of the people's stubbornness, rebellion and fear, God's desire was to show mercy. Moses may have spent a long time in preparation for his divinely appointed task, but God had his methods to work humility, faith and courage in Moses so that his servant would not trust in himself, but obey God. As a result, His appointed leader delivered a nation of people from slavery.

Esther's painful transition began when she was orphaned at a young age. She was selected to take part in a beauty contest to be a potential replacement to the current queen, Vashti. Esther was selected to be queen and was elevated from a lowly peasant girl to a position of royalty, but she was unaware at the time how much it would cost her. She kept her Jewish identity a secret at her cousin Mordecai's urging. In time, Mordecai learned of a secret plot to destroy the Jews as a result of the king's trusted advisor, Haman. Mordecai urged Esther to intervene and plead for the lives of her people before the king. This was a dangerous risk, as one could not appear before the king uninvited, or the result could be a death sentence. Esther put her own life at risk in order to see her Jewish brothers and sisters spared from a slaughter planned by the enemy. This took careful planning and preparation to win the favor of the king and overthrow the plot of destruction, but as we see from her story, God placed her into the king's chamber at the precise moment, when Esther had been given strategy. God's favor on Esther helped her secure the victory for her people because she was willing to consider the lives of others over her own safety and security. Esther's bravery saved the Jews from destruction.

The Old Testament prophet, Jeremiah, was another individual that was called by God before he was even born. Jeremiah was acutely aware that the call of God had been placed upon his life even before his birth. The word of the Lord came to Jeremiah, "Before I formed you in the womb I knew you, before you were born I set you apart. I appointed you as a prophet to the nations."(Jeremiah 1:5-6) Jeremiah understood that he was part of God's divine plan to proclaim God's message to the nation at a specific time in history. Jeremiah's transition into his calling as a prophet was not an easy one. It came at a time when God's people were in a state of backsliding and moral and spiritual decay. Jeremiah's message was one of warning and judgment, calling people to repentance, but the people rebelled by beating him and imprisonment. He faced a great deal of hostility, opposition and persecution, but in spite of these things he remained faithful to speak God's messages. Many times, Jeremiah felt alone in his mission, and he was even thrown in a pit full of mud to die. God rescued His servant, though, and Jeremiah's faithfulness is a tremendous testimony to God's covenant that continues to inspire and encourage people today.

David acknowledged in Psalms 139:16, "You saw me before I was born and scheduled each day of my life before I began to breathe. Every day was recorded in your book."(Living Bible). David's transition began when the prophet Samuel showed up one day unexpectedly and anointed him with oil to become the next reigning king, as a replacement for King Saul. At the time, David was just a young shepherd boy, but God's greater purposes were already at work to prepare him from being a humble shepherd to becoming the King of Israel. David's family saw a young lad, and like Joseph, his brothers seemed to despise him, but God saw David's potential to be His leader and future king. David spent many years as a fugitive as he endured Saul's jealousy and many attempts to murder him before he could come into position as Saul's replacement. David faced many challenges and trials, and he had some noteworthy failures along the way, but he remained faithful to God. David gained experience through adversity that prepared him for his leadership role and he became one of the greatest leaders in Israel's history.

We have each been made by the hand of God with a divine purpose in mind. He appointed the very place we would live, the journey of our life mapped out ahead of time. We all have different assignments to fulfill because we are each a unique part of God's master plan to touch others for the Kingdom of God. There are many experiences, times of adversity, trials and testing that will be a part of our training and preparation to ready us for God's divine purpose. During these times, when we cannot see the bigger picture, it is important not to lose hope. Although it may seem there is no purpose to things we go through, God will not waste anything. He will use every bit of our pain and adversity to learn from it and grow. There is always purpose through the darkness. God has allowed us to be raised up at this particular time in history and he has given us a task that is divinely tailored just for us. He has cleared the ground for our generation to be rooted in His Promised Land and fill the earth with His glory. Our assignments will utilize all our past experiences, our skills, abilities and the gifts he has placed in us. He does have a wonderful plan for each of us! We may not always share His perspective on things that are good for us; nevertheless, He will turn things for our good as we submit to His authority. We must learn to submit to His authority to be in authority. This is a principle of scripture. (Matthew 8:5-13). The question is whether or not we will say yes to His plan for our life.

The children of Israel saw the acts of God. They saw many signs and miracles, but it didn't change them. I would hope that if I personally witnessed the parting of the Red Sea that delivered me from death, I would have the faith to continue to believe in God's power and faithfulness. Sadly though, the demonstrations of God's power are not enough for some people. It's only in His presence that we are truly changed. The Israelites did not want to know God. They just wanted the convenience of looking to their leader to tell them what to do. Subsequently, they didn't trust God. After all, how can you trust someone you have no relationship with? Steeped in unbelief and driven by their needs, they lacked any personal relationship with God. They had eyes that were blinded to see in the spirit, deaf ears that could not hear what the spirit was saying, and a mind that simply could not comprehend what God was doing.

The encouragement in scripture for every generation is, "No eye has seen, no ear has heard; no mind has conceived of what God has prepared for those that love Him." (1 Corinthians 2:9). Human wisdom is limited to what can be observed in the natural realm. Our brains want answers, but we need to be careful because sometimes our minds try to come up with an answer based on incomplete information. We rely on our natural senses to form a picture, concept or idea that can be worked out in our minds with the details and knowledge that is available to us. However, human intellect cannot tap into the supernatural realm where God's Spirit reveals His secrets. We must rely on the help of the Holy Spirit to understand the thoughts of God, and this only comes through the mind of Christ. That is why people who rely on their natural way of thinking reject spiritual truth and think it is foolishness. They simply cannot comprehend it because their minds are not renewed by His Spirit. God's wisdom requires faith to believe what He shows us through revelation. That is why the scripture says we can't even imagine what God has stored up for us. He wants us to stop trying to think with our natural man and come up higher, entering His presence through worship and prayer, so that we can access the secrets of God. When you feel stuck without understanding or going in circles, asking the same questions of God, ask yourself if you are trying to figure things out with your natural mind. When we do, the result is often confusion because God hasn't spoken yet about the thing we are trying to figure out. Are you spending time with the Holy Spirit in the secret place? With a better covenant and better promises God has made the way for those who love Him to come into His presence. We can find grace in the time of our need. We will find that God is there, waiting to have fellowship with us.

Challenge #1 - Knowing His Ways

There are three challenges that my wife and I have experienced as God prepared us for that place of ministry. The first is the need to know His ways. Isaiah 55:8 says, "For My thoughts are not your thoughts, neither my ways your ways." The Bible tells us in Psalm 103:7, "He made known His ways to Moses, His acts unto the children of Israel." We know that God prepares the way and that He establishes a route on a determined path. He works tirelessly to clear the obstacles out of our way. When we talk about God clearing out obstacles, it is primarily concerning our character to prepare us for our destination, so we are essentially talking about the process of sanctification. Sanctification is the process by which God transforms us into the image of Christ. This process involves the removal of character deficits or obstacles that hinder our spiritual growth and prevent us from walking on the Highway of Holiness mentioned in Isaiah 35:8-10. This passage describes a road that is reserved for the people of God, and it is a road that is free from obstacles and dangers. The passage also talks about how the redeemed will walk on this road and how they will experience joy and gladness. The removal of character deficits can take many forms, such as pride, selfishness, dishonesty, anger, bitterness, and unforgiveness to name a few. These things can be obstacles that prevent us from experiencing the joy and gladness that Isaiah talks about. They can also hinder our ability to serve God and others effectively.

To clear out these obstacles, God often allows us to go through difficult circumstances and trials. These trials can be painful, but they serve a purpose in our lives. They help us to see our weaknesses and to rely on God's strength to overcome them. As we submit to God's work in our lives, He can use these trials to shape our character and transform us into the image of Christ. There is a joy and peace of mind that comes from knowing God takes His time in removing the things that can trip us up and lead us into things that were once a cause for shame and failure. That is not a road we want to walk on and that is not our destination. Let God deliver you so that the stumbling blocks are taken out and you gain the advantage of wisdom, then you can have confidence towards your future.

He has prepared us and prepared the city of our destination. As with Joshua and the children of Israel, the way is not always clear. I'm sure the Israelites wondered how on earth they were going to cross the Jordan River during the time that it was near flood stage and overflowing its banks. That was something they could not understand with their natural reasoning. Yet, at the appointed time God gave the command. His Spirit made the way clear, and they walked over on dry ground. There was not an inch of water and they didn't sink up to their ankles in the mud. The scripture says they walked over on dry ground. Moses and the children of Israel experienced a similar miracle when God parted the Red Sea. When we are stuck, then we are waiting on a supernatural intervention from God. His path to freedom remained hidden until the precise moment it was needed, but it was there the entire time. Moses saw a dead end. It wasn't until he extended his faith and began to prophesy to the dead end that the future opened up and the road became visible. There are times when God restrains our eyes from seeing what we need to see or the next step we are to take until the time is right, but don't let unbelief try to convince you it doesn't exist. Maintain an attitude of faith and confidence towards the Lord. God can do anything to get us to our desired destination right on time. Pray for whoever or whatever is involved with the intervention you need. Sometimes you are waiting to meet a divine connection that will be another piece of the puzzle. Pray for God to help you cross paths and have the conversations that need to happen to move you along. Ask God to shift what needs to be shifted, to extend His power to move what needs to move, to open the right doors, and to release His Spirit to put the missing pieces in place.

God did something new through Moses' successor, Joshua. In Moses' days, the people learned to keep their eyes on their leader. When that era was over, the people learned a new way to follow God. They had to look to the priest with the Ark of the Covenant to lead them because the ark contained the presence of God. In Joshua chapter three, the people were told to keep their eyes on the Ark, and when they saw it they were to move out from their positions and follow it. Joshua was a skilled military leader that knew the strategies of God, and led the Israelites into battle against their enemies as they learned to follow God's presence. Joshua was a strong but fair leader and led them on many victorious campaigns. Joshua was not there to advance his own agenda; He was there to lead God's people in the conquest of the land, but there was a strong emphasis on the fact that it was their obedience that won the victories. So it is with us today. God will give us strategies that help us eradicate our enemies, but it can only be accomplished through our obedience. We must be willing to lay down our own agendas in order to follow God and advance His kingdom purposes.

Transition is a hard place to be, there's no doubt about it. You know you can't go back to the old way of life, but you don't know how to move forward, either. It's much like a woman in labor. When transition hits it can be very uncomfortable because that baby must be born. You've been pregnant with a promise, a hope, a vision for your future, and when the labor pains begin, a process that has been in motion for a long time must come to a point of resolution one way or another. " Shall I bring to the time of birth and not cause delivery? " says the Lord. Shall I who cause delivery shut up the womb? " says your God. (Isaiah 66:9) Many people are in that place now and they feel that they've been expecting far too long. It's a painful process but the reward will be worth it. Keep laboring in prayer until the Lord brings about the birth of your promise. It will happen! A woman in transition about to give birth often feels as if she wants to give up, but she can't. Her body won't let her. An involuntary process takes over, compelling her body to force that child out of the womb and into the light of day. The mother's body actually rejects the baby so that the child can live, but the child is forced to live outside of what it's known as its comfort zone. So it is in the Spirit, too. The effect of our long seasons of waiting and praying eventually compel all of Heaven to set the stage for the birth of God's promise. It can be a tumultuous time of change, but if we resist the changes that must occur, even though some may be painful and unexpected, it will only serve to delay the birth or perhaps cause it to be prematurely aborted. Sometimes we too, must go through a process where we are rejected and are forced to leave everything familiar. Don't despise the ones that reject you, because although rejection or closed doors can be difficult and painful experiences, they are also opportunities in disguise to lead us into God's will. When things don't work out in one place, there are reasons for it. God may not tell you why, but trust Him. There have been times when we would get our hopes up then suddenly things would fall apart. Those things can be very discouraging and disappointing, but God used those things to continue to say, 'No, not that,' and redirect us. It was only after the fact that other things became more clear and we were grateful God got involved when He did. I think of the many times when we would suddenly be forced to move when the owners of the properties we rented would suddenly put the house up for sale. It was at times frustrating and disappointing because we didn't stay in one location very long. God would close certain doors and open a new one to direct us into new locations, where we would meet new people we wouldn't have met otherwise. Each time, He would make it known that it was His favor opening a new door. Rejection, closed doors and disappointments can force you to go a different direction so that you find the right people and the right place where God births something new in your life. He knows who we are to birth with and the exact location for that birth to come forth in health and safety. You can trust him to guide you to the right place. The Holy Spirit hovers over us to oversee the birthing process. His dream is bigger than our personal desires. His dream will touch others with new life, salvation, healing and deliverance. The fulfillment of the promise often touches many more lives than we could ever imagine. We are designed to work as a team with others. This is how the Lord releases the Kingdom of God on the earth.

You may find yourself with many unanswered questions. How is the Holy Spirit going to open the door for ministry? How can I know where to find that door that leads to the new thing God is waiting to birth? The promise of our Father becomes our guide and instructor in His ways. In Exodus 23: 20, Israel is assured that God is sending an angel ahead of them to make sure they arrive at their destination safely. "See, I am sending an angel ahead of you to guard you along the way and to bring you to the place I have prepared." So many times we get caught up in trying to figure out how to find the right door, instead of focusing on what opens the door. When you use the right key, the door will open.

The disciples had the same concerns. Jesus performed amazing miracles in their midst. No one had displayed such power, signs and wonders. When Jesus prepared them for His departure, he reassured them that he needed to leave in order that the promise of the Father, the Comforter, would come. When the Spirit of Truth comes, He will guide you into all truth. The Holy Spirit will pass on what he has heard from the Father and He will tell you about the future. In John 9:27, Jesus healed a certain blind man who was later treated harshly by the Pharisees. He responded to their interrogation by asking a simple question. "Do you want to become His disciples too?" They answered him with insults and said, "We are disciples of Moses! We know God spoke to Moses, but we don't know where **He** comes from," (Referring to Jesus). It is very typical for those who have loyalties to their denominations, pastors, churches, or philosophies to have their eyes on their theology or certain individuals rather than on the work of the Holy Spirit.

Sometimes they are the voice of God to us, but at other times they may not be. It's important to know how to tell the difference. Discerning when God is speaking through a person and when that person is speaking from their own natural wisdom can be a challenging task. Here are some suggestions that may help you discern:

1. Pray: Ask God for guidance and wisdom to discern whether the message is from Him or not.Not every thought that sounds like it could be God is from Him. Not every door that opens is from the Lord. Sometimes the enemy will bait the hook with what sounds like a great deal to make you think it's the Lord, but it's not. The enemy would like to give you his thoughts to lead you in the wrong direction, away from God's plan, but he also knows that you will not follow his voice unless it sounds like it is the voice of the Lord. Satan masquerades as a counterfeit. If the enemy cannot move you in the direction he wants with one tactic, he will try another. Make sure you pray for confirmation and have peace about things before you make decisions.

2. Check it against the Bible: The Bible is the word of God, and it is the ultimate authority for Christians. Check the message against what the Bible says. If the message contradicts the Bible, then it is likely not from God.

3. Seek counsel: Seek counsel from trusted and mature Christians who can help you discern the message. They may have insights or perspectives from their own history. However, with that said, it is imperative that even with the wisdom of mature Christians, sometimes it is still not the word of the Lord for you at that moment or for that particular situation. At different times in my life, I have had many people try to influence my decisions contrary to what I knew God was leading me into. Taking steps of faith will always require a risk, and others may not understand what God is asking of you.

4. Test the Spirit: The Bible warns us to test every spirit to see if it is from God (1 John 4:1). Do not automatically take the counsel of someone that is unsaved and not walking with God, because they will likely offer worldly counsel. The Bible says that worldly wisdom is sensual and influenced by a demonic origin. The world does not have the answers we need. God does. What is their walk of faith like? Have they taken some risky steps of faith in their own life? Ask them to share their testimonies. It is not wise to take counsel from someone that has not walked things out with God. Experience produces wisdom, but you need godly wisdom.

5. Look for fruit: Jesus said, "You will recognize them by their fruits" (Matthew 7:16). Look for evidence of the fruit of the Spirit in the person's life (love, joy, peace, patience, kindness, goodness, faithfulness, gentleness, and self-control) and see if the message they are sharing is consistent with their character.

6. Don't focus on the people or things that represent your personal pot and confinements. We must learn to follow the leading and direction that the Holy Spirit provides rather than advice from those who may have mixed motives for their counsel.

Jesus told Nicodemus, one of Moses's disciples, that to be born again and led of the Spirit is to understand the power and mystery of the wind. "The wind blows wherever it pleases. You hear its sound but you cannot tell where it comes from or where it is going. So it is with everyone born of the Spirit." (John 3:8). In the upper room the disciples were gathered in one accord. Suddenly, a sound like the blowing of a violent wind came from heaven and filled the whole house where they were sitting. That promise from the Father changed history and the lives of all who were present.

When the Holy Spirit outpouring took place in Pensacola, Florida at Brownsville in 1995, the revival changed the lives of thousands and thousands of people. God has come down and brought revival to Argentina, Toronto, Azusa Street in Los Angeles, and a variety of other places throughout history. There are currently many different manifestations of His Spirit touching college campuses throughout our nation. The Holy Spirit is moving mightily in many nations. When the winds of revival blow, miracles, signs, and wonders take place. God often uproots and replants people as a result of Him moving in their lives. We don't know where the Holy Spirit will visit next, but people are hungry for God. When God shows up, he comes to the hungry, seeking heart. He clears the ground for the planting of God's vine. He waters and pours out from heaven the divine rain of His mercies for the growth of His planting. Like Joshua and the children of Israel, we can't cross the Jordan without His presence. We can't expect to see the walls of our fortified cities come down without the guidance of the Spirit. The Spirit will show us the way to confirm God's direction through prophecy, vision and dreams. Shortly after we began attending a certain church in Pensacola, the church hosted a prophetic conference with Pastor/Evangelist Kevin McAnulty. We were praying, fasting, and asking the Lord to confirm his purpose for coming to Pensacola. In the second meeting Pastor Kevin picked us out of the auditorium of over 400 people and started to prophesy over our lives. He told us that the enemy was not the one to bring us to Florida, but God had brought us out of the old so as to take us into the new. Several times he stressed the fact that it wasn't the enemy that broke us out, it was God. He told us that God had to change our wineskins in order to fill us with his new wine, and that we were going to be sent back to the nations. Sometimes a person has to leave their past behind in order to receive the Kingdom of God. My wife and I were blessed and assured of God's direction. We have both had many dreams of God's purposes for our lives. God taught us to listen for His voice and to be attentive to the Spirit. Knowing God's ways is learning to listen, submit, and follow Him even when He works outside of our understanding, but much of this also involves knowing His heart. If we don't understand His heart towards us, the difficulties of being in transition can cause us to misjudge who He is and distort our image of Him.

Challenge #2 - Learning to Wait

The next challenge is learning how to wait on God. This is one of the hardest things to do. It is also one of the most humbling. It is hard at times to fight the frustration during the delay. There are so many times when we think we're ready to be about our Father's business doing something bigger or more satisfying, but all God says is 'not yet.' It is a time when God develops the fruit of patience. It is also equally difficult not to grow weary but God has his purposes and He is not obligated to disclose all of them. My wife and I have prayed, fasted, worshiped, cried out, quoted scriptures, rebuked the enemy, broke curses, danced, and marched over territory while declaring God's promises. We have anointed everything we knew with oil. We still heard the word, wait. A person can tire themselves out trying to get God to move, but He still has his set time. Does that mean sit around and watch TV while you wait for God to show up? No! Waiting is the most active thing a person can do, but it also comes with a peace of simply enjoying where you're at and enjoying fellowship with the Lord while you wait. If you can do nothing else, then learn to love Him where you're at.

When my wife and I moved to the Pensacola area, we asked God to direct us to the right church. Although we immensely enjoyed the ministry of Brownsville Assembly and the Friday night renewal services, God directed us to a different church closer to where we lived. It wasn't long before we knew it felt like home. Not long afterwards, we met with the pastor and submitted to his leadership.

Overcoming Church Hurt

Please allow me to share some thoughts with you regarding submission to authority and pastoral covering. Laura and I were apprehensive in trusting new relationships because of our former experiences. In the past, we had seen church leadership and ministerial organizations as the means of control and competition. We also knew what it was like to be mistreated by those that abuse their authority and were wounded by their actions. For many people, their faith is deeply intertwined with their experience of community. When certain leaders or that community fails to live up to their expectations or causes harm, it can be difficult to separate those negative experiences from their understanding of God. When people are hurt by a church or religious organization, it is understandable that they may feel hurt and betrayed. However, it is important to remember that God is not the one who hurts us. It can be helpful to define abusive, toxic, or unloving behavior from others for what it is because that can help distinguish in a person's mind that it wasn't God that hurt or mistreated them. We should not blame the entire faith community or God for certain individuals that have bad fruit in their lives. It is important to separate the wrong behavior of certain individuals from the true character of the God that loves us. Our Father and His precious Holy Spirit love justice, humility and mercy. People that have been hurt and disappointed as a result of church hurt may feel like withdrawing from others. There is a natural tendency towards self-preservation and the inclination to keep yourself at an emotional distance. Multitudes are displaced from the church for just those reasons.

Perhaps you are reading this book and can identify with the same feelings and experiences. You are not alone. Many people have had negative experiences, but that certainly does not apply to all pastoral relationships. It is imperative that you overcome those feelings and get healed from old wounds. If you don't, any unhealed wounds becomes an automatic open door to the enemy, granting him access to everything you have. It is important to be able to recognize your own triggers that stem from a lack of healing. Emotional pain can cause unreasonable sensitivity so that your responses come from anger, a tendency to dominate or control others. The unhealed issues will cause you to not be able to hear what others are trying to communicate. The pain that comes from rejection, fear of failure, fear of disappointing others, or feelings of disrespect become triggers that will corrupt your communication with others and cause you to make decisions that will negatively affect all your relationships and the decisions you make. Nothing good can come from trying to lead yourself, your family or others from a place of pain. Unhealed wounds stem from unforgiveness and judgments against others, and unless you get healed, you will end up reproducing hurt and offense in others. Unforgiveness will block your prayers and keep you from receiving God's best. Unforgiveness is such an important issue to God that it prevents your access to heaven. Satan knows that you cannot fulfill your destiny with unhealed wounds and trust issues. He will plot and scheme against you to take advantage of you and keep you blinded by self-deception. If Satan can keep you locked up in your hurts and offenses, he's gained the power to hinder your ability to bear good fruit and receive answers to prayer. Unforgiveness, insecurity, and wounding will also keep you from trusting other relationships and frustrate your ability to be intimate with the Holy Spirit. We all need the benefit of healthy, godly relationships. They help keep our lives in balance and offer a healthy support system of people that will love us, pray for us, and help us stay accountable in our walk with God. There are people that understand your pain and can relate to the wounded. The Holy Spirit will bring people into your life who will have words of comfort and healing. They may be spiritual leaders or the neighbors next door. God created us to need one another, and by his design we need the gifts He has put in others, because it is the gifts of the Holy Spirit that help us heal. The ministry of the Holy Spirit and many wonderful people in the body of Christ were so instrumental in our healing and restoration.

The Necessity of Healing

The children of Israel were going to be planted into the Promised Land. Before they were to proceed however, the old way of thinking and the old order of things had to die in the wilderness. Joshua, God's leader to bring Israel into their inheritance, was instructed by the Lord to have those who had grown up in the wilderness circumcised. The whole first generation disobeyed God and had forfeited their promises because they allowed fear, insecurity, and unbelief to rule over their minds, which led them into rebellion. If we listen to the voice of fear, it will always lead us into the wrong decisions. The people refused to fight for what God wanted to give them! They just could not overcome their limiting mindsets even though God had set them free from many years of hard bondage and slavery. In order to give the children the right of inheritance that their elders and ancestors walked away from, God waited until a new generation came on the scene. Joshua had the males circumcised according to God's word. At that time the Lord said to Joshua, "Make flint knives and circumcise the Israelites again. So Joshua made flint knives and circumcised the Israelites at Gibeth Haaroloff. Now this is why he did so: all those who came out of Egypt - all the men of military age - died in the wilderness on the way after leaving Egypt. All the people that came out had been circumcised, but all the people born in the wilderness during the journey from Egypt had not. The Israelites had moved about in the wilderness 40 years until all the men who were of military age when they left Egypt had died, since they had not obeyed the Lord. For the Lord had sworn to them that they would not see the land he had solemnly promised their ancestors to give us, a land flowing with milk and honey. So he raised up their sons in their place, and these were the ones Joshua circumcised. They were still uncircumcised because they had not been circumcised on the way. And after the whole nation had been circumcised, *they remained where they were in camp until they were healed,* (Emphasis mine).Then the Lord said to Joshua, "Today I have rolled away the reproach of Egypt from you. So the place has been called Gilgal to this day."(Joshua 5:2-9).

Circumcision was an outward sign in their flesh that marked them as different from other nations, and it also spoke of sanctification of their heart and life. They were a people set apart by the Lord to be an example to other nations. What is interesting in verse 8 is that they had to stay where they were until they were healed. This is a principle of God's ways. If we feel stuck on hold and it feels like you can't seem to move forward, it is often due to a need for healing and deliverance in some area of your heart and life. There are no shortcuts with God. He simply will not open certain doors for us until we do things His way. We don't get to bury the pain, ignore the promptings of the

Holy Spirit, and pretend that we are ready for the new thing when we haven't yet dealt with the things from the past. The Lord wants to take away the reproach - the things that have resulted in us carrying around shame, condemnation, sorrow or other negative emotions from past events. He waits in order to cleanse us from things that hinder our ability to bear good fruit, because He doesn't want us defiling others with the wrong sort of messages. He waits until we can see ourselves the way He sees us, as a man or woman that has learned humility but also knows that they are called by God to fulfill His mandate in the earth.

My favorite scripture during this time has been Hebrews 6:12. "...imitate those who through faith and patience inherit what has been promised." Abraham, through patient endurance, inherited his promise. James 1:4 also says, "Perseverance must finish its work so that you may be mature and complete, not lacking anything. " Experience is the only way we can truly understand the revelation of these scriptures. Light bulbs will go off in your Spirit in reference to the knowledge of His will, but it's only through the test that the knowledge is perfected into our character. No man, of his own ability, changes himself. Man cannot change the human heart. Only God can orchestrate the right kind of circumstances that have the capacity to change a man's character. Almighty God, Creator of the universe, desires to share His nature with us. Being a son of a pastor, there were times in my rebellious teenage years when people would say, "You may look and sound like your dad, but you don't act much like him." God will wait until we look and act a bit more like him so that when the breakthrough comes our character doesn't shoot us in the foot. God doesn't want to give us a blessing only to have us lose it due to a lack of integrity. He weeds out corruption by refining our nature, and works integrity and humility into us so that we are adequately prepared to properly steward the blessings He has for us. That is why we count it all joy when we face trials of many kinds. It is a time of trusting Him to work things out on our behalf. During times of waiting, we must fight unbelief and maintain a right confession so that we can resist the tendency to take matters into our own hands. There are times when we feel as though God has forgotten about us, and we think we've waited long enough. We consider taking situations into our own hands and devising our own plans, but to do so could be a big mistake. I could list the many examples in the Bible of people who failed to wait on God and reap the consequences of their impatience and disobedience, but instead let me encourage your faith.

Isaiah 40:31 declares that as we wait on God our strength will be renewed as the eagle's. When storms or violent winds come, eagles catch the wind under their wings and fly above the storm. God wants us to rise above the storms as well so He sends the wind of his Spirit to lift us up and carry us above our troubles. We experience this when we worship him. The power of His presence during worship magnifies His abilities and His power, which comforts us. It reminds us just how capable he is to handle all the situations in our lives. Laura and I like to go to the beach to feel the wind in our face and look upon the majesty of His creation. The ocean is a magnificent creation and there is so much going on beneath the surface that cannot be seen by the naked eye. It's a good reminder that there is also so much more going on in the Spirit that we are unaware of. The beach is a good place to go for a change of atmosphere. It restores us to the right frame of mind. Laura tells me that when she looks at the magnitude of what God created with just his word, it puts things back into perspective. You may enjoy a special place of your own, and it's good to take a break when you feel out of sorts or need an emotional reset. Thank God for the strength He imparts to us! During times when the weariness is overwhelming, He carries us on his wings. "It is good to wait quietly for the salvation of the Lord." (Lamentations 3:26). Be patient, God is making everything ready. He is at work behind the scenes. He never slumbers or sleeps and He isn't an absent-minded professor. He's thinking about your situation and taking care of all the details. God is clearing the field; the soil is made ready and the rain for the harvest is there. When you wait on God and you become desperate for Him, you become ruined only for him. Nothing else will do. Nothing else will cleanse and empower you. When He lifts us up from our humble state we cry out, "Here I am, send me." At His appointed time, we are sent to His ordained place in His prescribed way.

Challenge #3 - Resting in His Promises

The next challenge is learning to rest in his promises. This can be the biggest challenge for people, especially men. I know it is for me. I want to plan and execute an answer to all the obstacles. My mind never stops thinking about the possibilities of every opportunity. The problem with an overthinker is doing more or saying more than God asks of us. He looks for people that will say and do exactly what He wants; no more, no less. In our exuberance we can be traveling on our journey and be so excited about getting to our destiny that we miss the turnoff. Or, like most men, be so determined that we know the way and be too proud to admit we're lost. We never want to presume that we will succeed only on our merits or assume He has spoken if He hasn't. To walk out in faith, like Peter did when he stepped off the boat, we need a sure word from the Lord. He wants us to be like Peter and say, "Lord, bid me to come." He wants us to have confidence and be at rest from our own ambitions so that we can boldly declare that God was the one that opened the door. God sent me. God is with me. If not, the enemy will beat you down and you can end up scratching your head and asking yourself, "Where did He go?" In Luke 2:44, Joseph and Mary presumed Jesus was with them when He was actually back at Jerusalem attending to His Father's business. It's very easy to assume that God is with us when we are doing what seems right.

We had been in Florida several years when we knew we heard Him speak about being committed to a change. I ended up sowing my livelihood for the sake of the kingdom, which was a very scary decision. Although Laura and I both knew we had heard from God, it had tremendous ramifications. People did not understand what was happening with us and some people told us, "God wouldn't tell you to do something like that." Or, "You're being irresponsible. You need to provide for your family." We second guessed ourselves so many times because God took us down a path that made absolutely no sense and it cost us dearly, but we knew what we heard from the Lord. Once the decision was made to follow God, work just dried up. I tried desperately to get something going again for work, but it was very scarce. It was very difficult just trying to survive. We ended up losing our home and life became very unstable for a while. My youngest son had just been born, and we found ourselves in a difficult financial storm. Nothing really made any sense why we were going through such a difficult time. I've heard transition is somewhat like being in a hallway between two doors. One has closed behind you, but the other one hasn't opened yet. A hallway is a very narrow place, and we sure felt the squeeze that led up to birth pangs.

During this time, we got down to our last meal and Laura said we should sow it into someone else that also had a dire need. So, we went downtown and went to look for some homeless people to feed. At that point, we were desperate to operate by a kingdom principle and we thought of the story of Elijah's widow in first king 17: 7 - 16.

60

Laura felt it was a God inspired idea, so off we went. That sacrificial act set off a domino effect that we never could have seen coming. Ladies from our life group found out what we had done and they wanted to help. We took food down to the park each week to feed people. The third week we were there, the police showed up to ask us to leave because we didn't have a permit, but there were also about 50 kids from a school field trip eating their sack lunches and they didn't have a permit, and no one asked them to leave. A reporter showed up as well. He blended in with the homeless so we didn't realize at first that he was a journalist. He asked a few questions as to why we were there, but the next day his article hit the front page and the blog responses went crazy. We found ourselves in the middle of a heated battle between the downtown business owners, the homeless, the city manager's office and many others who had issues with the homeless population. A day or two later, we got a phone call and were asked to come to the city manager's office, but we were not told why. What we found out was that the comments from the newspaper article prompted the ACLU to get involved and start making inquiries, and the mayor's office was notified that the situation seemed to be escalating. He wanted all the phone calls to stop, so he told the city manager to 'make it go away.' While I was there, I heard the Holy Spirit tell me to ask if we could hold an outreach in the premier park downtown - the same one we had gotten kicked out of two days earlier! To my surprise, the City Manager said yes, and then I decided to ask if there was a place we could feed the homeless every week. He said he would work on it, and about a week later we were called to the City Manager' office again. This time, when we got there we entered a room with all the heads of various departments present around a round table. Laura and I thought we must be in trouble for something because the heads of police, the fire department, parks and recreation, code enforcement and many others were there. But, to our surprise, they were there to help serve us and our request for a park to feed the homeless was granted. They waived all the permits and fees, and asked how they could be of service. Somehow, I found myself divinely placed as a peacekeeper between the City Manager's office and an advocate to the homeless of Pensacola. God miraculously orchestrated a chain of events that brought many people in the body of Christ together outside the walls of the church. There was a lot of opposition too, though. God was absolutely in the middle of everything going on. So many miracles happened that never would have occurred had we not said yes when God told us to sow the business. We knew that for certain. Our faith was stretched in a glorious way, and there was no reason to believe that God would want us to stop the good works we had begun. We continued the park ministry for well over a year and a half. Imagine our surprise when nothing else came together, and I mean, nothing. I had gone from having my own successful flooring business to barely being able to scrape up any work at all. It was so natural for me to think that God would have us continue in the same place as where He was growing the ministry that it never occurred to us that things weren't working financially because He had another plan. He had changed directions without us understanding it. I struggled to make things work because I was trying to provide for my family. It never occurred to me to ask Him if He was relocating us. One day an Apostolic leader by the name of Ken Malone prayed for Laura to have the revelation of why we were going through such difficulty, and he asked one simple question. "Are you sure God isn't trying to realign you?" When we asked the right question, God answered and confirmed that He was preparing to move us in a different direction, back to California. We surely did not expect that! Always remember to check in with God from time to time, even if you think you know the answer. Assuming we know God's plans or His timetable can have disastrous results if we don't keep up with where He's going. Remember, He leads; we follow. Sometimes we struggle far longer than we have to simply because we fail to ask the right questions sooner.

Discerning the Activity of the Holy Spirit

The Holy Spirit wants to bring transformation to our lives and our community. Transformation in our communities must begin with hearts yielded to the Holy Spirit. Our Spiritual health is determined by the activity of the Holy Spirit. If the Holy Spirit is not active and ministering in our lives, other spirits will fill that void. Sometimes God is not involved at all in the things that people are doing even when they may believe that they are doing what they feel they are supposed to do. The Spirit could be absent from our activities and sadly most would go on with business as usual. Different people may have different interpretations and experiences regarding the presence and work of the Holy Spirit, but here are some things to consider.

1. Supernatural manifestations: The Holy Spirit can bring supernatural manifestations such as healings, miracles, prophetic words, and tongues. If there is a lack of such manifestations, some may interpret that the Holy Spirit is not actively present or allowed freedom to minister through you. Are people being prayed for? Do you see the evidence of those that are touched by the flow of the Spirit? Are the gifts of the Holy Spirit released to bring prophetic words to others? Perhaps most importantly, are others drawn in by the life-giving flow of God's Spirit? Wherever Jesus went, people were attracted to his teaching and ministry because it witnessed to them that the power of God was real, and God was among them. So, why do we settle for less? Why do we settle for ordinary when we could have the supernatural? We cannot afford to let our traditional way of doing things replace the presence of God. If the priority is not on cultivating a place for God's presence through worship and intercession, we will substitute other things that have no power to transform us. Those who have a close relationship with Him will sense if God is really involved or if the dove has quietly flown away.

2. Supernatural love: The Bible says that the greatest of all our efforts is love. We could have faith that moves mountains, but if we fail to show love, we are nothing. If we have given everything we have away but lack love, we have gained nothing. Faith expressing itself through love is what truly matters. Everything we do, everything we are, everything that is expressed through the Holy Spirit is through love.

3. Supernatural unity: Being in one accord brings about supernatural manifestations, prayers of agreement are answered, people are set free. The Holy Spirit has room to move.

4. Supernatural prayer: If we do not sense the Fathers presence, we won't be interested in prayer. If the Holy Spirit is not present we do not believe there will be answers. If Jesus is not in the room we are lost.

5. Supernatural fruit: You shall know them by their fruit. The Lord wants a fruitful vine that will be healthy and producing. A vine that does not produce is cut down and thrown into the fire.

6. Supernatural strength: When the Holy Spirit is replaced by human effort, then it is not Him ministering. We are likely under the influence of a spirit of control and manipulation, which is witchcraft. There may be evidence of a religious spirit, or legalism at work. An atmosphere controlled by the wrong spirit will feel oppressive, heavy and empty. When a wrong spirit has infiltrated your life or ministry, it causes a disturbed feeling in one's spirit. You may not know exactly why, but there's a lack of peace and something feels 'off.' The enemy tries to hide within the

community of believers, which makes it more difficult to discern. It may feel like you're being watched by some unseen entity, or you may find it difficult to concentrate, pray or hear from God. You may suddenly feel anxious, fearful, depressed, or experience other emotions that are not typical for you. Confusion and mental fatigue are also telltale signs that a spirit of confusion is attacking your mind. Witchcraft takes root through unhealed offense and brokenness, and operates through pride. It supplants God's authority with the desire to lord over and dominate others, and to derail destinies. Only the enemy working through the fleshly desires of others attempts to control people, often through manipulation of their emotions. The Holy Spirit never violates our free will or acts oppressive towards people. A spirit of witchcraft will sow strife and produce contention, accuse, offend, and break relationships. A spirit of error will cause believers to question their freedom and authority in Christ and come under false yokes. The wrong use of scripture uses guilt, condemnation and intimidation to convince people to submit to a spirit of false authority.

Divination, which is a spirit of witchcraft that counterfeits real prophecy, will also attempt to disguise itself as a legitimate spiritual gift. This is how the enemy works within our lives. It mimics Christian behavior so as to operate unnoticed within the atmosphere of a supposedly 'safe environment,' hoping to take advantage of the unsuspecting. Divination comes from the spirit of python. Pythons constrict and suffocate their victims through squeezing and constriction, and this is what the python spirit attempts to do in the church. It slowly constricts the movement of the Holy Spirit until the church is chained, then it comes in as a counterfeit to the gift of the Holy Spirit, which brings defilement. The 'prophecy' from this spirit does come by supernatural revelation, but it does not come from God. It comes from the enemy. We know the enemy is also a liar, so the source cannot be trusted, because there will always be a demonic agenda attached to the words. No matter how accurate the prophecy may be, it will often appeal to a person's pride or ego, or attempt to defile the recipient through bitterness, offense and disappointment when the words don't come to pass. This is because divination comes from a demonic origin. In contrast, a New Testament community of believers should represent what is genuinely the work of the Holy Spirit, evidenced by healthy, life-giving relationships, humility, sound doctrine, freedom, joy and peace. The gifts of the Spirit are used to edify and build up the community of believers.

7. Supernatural Freedom: Deliverance is part of the Great Commission Jesus gave to His followers. He told His disciples to cast out demons because freedom from oppressive spirits is vital to our spiritual health. There are many scriptures in the Bible that reference Jesus and the disciples casting out evil spirits. When the evil spirits were sent out of people, many received miracles of healing. Jesus made His promises available to us, but many people do not realize they may actually have some sort of an open door to the enemy through unconfessed sin or agreeing with lies. Demonic spirits always try to blind people to the work of the cross, and people need teaching and prophetic ministry to expose where the enemy has taken advantage of them so that they can get free and healed. Walking in deliverance is walking in freedom. Hold fast to the liberty that God has made available for you. Don't let yourself be deceived again to the point where you are entangled in bondage and under the wrong influences.

One of the ways the Spirit moves us into a place of rest is by quieting our soul. Zephaniah 3:17 says, "He will quiet you with his love, He will rejoice over you with singing." The word quiet means to be at rest in His love, or settle down in his love. The Apostle Paul said to be anxious for nothing, but make your request known, with thanksgiving.

God's love quiets the soul, and the revelation of His perfect love towards us casts out our fears. There's nothing more fulfilling and encouraging than to know that God loves me just the way I am. He is proud of me as his child and He always enjoys my fellowship with Him. My parents communicated that sentiment to me growing up. When I left home at 17 to attend Bible College, they were so pleased to hear from me and know that I was doing well. They loved me and missed me very much. When I would go back home for a visit they would love all over me and enjoy my company. It made no difference to them what my accomplishments and achievements were. They didn't welcome me because of my merits. They loved me and welcomed me because I was their son and they were my parents. I enjoyed being there so much not because of what they could give me, but because I loved being with them. I believe that is what you receive in God's rest when you quiet your soul. You also learn to trust Him. Proverbs 3:5 states, "Trust in the Lord with all your heart and lean not on your own understanding, but in all your ways acknowledge Him and He will direct your paths." When we rest in the Lord, we put our future in His hands and let Him be in control. He has cleared the way. He has prepared the soil. It's time for Him to plant us firmly in His open field.

ROOM TO GROW

Prayer for Healing the Heart and Memories

Dear Heavenly Father,

Thank you for being so involved in my life. Thank you for transforming the way I see things so that I can perceive things from the perspective of Your love for me. Lord, I surrender the hurt and disappointment I have carried towards myself and others. Please transform the pain into something good, redemptive and useful for the benefit of your kingdom. Lead me to a skilled, compassionate deliverance minister to assist with this process. Heal my memories, and help me remember the good about others. Help me forget the things the enemy has done to bring hurt, rejection and discouragement from others. When the enemy tries to remind me of something painful or turn it into an accusation towards myself, someone else, or you, remind me who I am at my core. Heal my disappointments and help me see them from a new perspective. I thank You, because I know You waste nothing and You will use every detail of my life and turn it for a good purpose. Open my eyes to view those things from your perspective and why they didn't work out. Help me remember I am yours, and I am safe in your presence. Help me to cast my cares upon you and rest in your presence. I yield my Spirit to you and trust you to work out the details of my future.

I ask You to shift the things that need to shift, and move whatever needs to be moved. Open the right doors for myself and others and let Your favor usher me into the doors You have for me. Father, give me increased discernment to know when something is a counterfeit of the enemy and what is truly from You. Confirm those things that are from You. In Jesus' name, amen.

ROOM TO GROW

CHAPTER FIVE
ROOT SYSTEMS

"You transplanted a vine out of Egypt; You drove out the nations **and planted it.**
You cleared the ground for it, and **it took root and filled the land."** Psalm 80:8,9

In the Bible, Jesus spoke about trees and their fruit in several instances. One of the most well-known passages can be found in Matthew chapter 7, where Jesus said: "Every good tree bears good fruit, but a bad tree bears bad fruit. A good tree cannot bear bad fruit, and a bad tree cannot bear good fruit. Every tree that does not bear good fruit is cut down and thrown into the fire. Thus, by their fruit you will recognize them." Jesus also used the analogy of a tree and its fruit to describe how people can be recognized by their actions and their true nature. In Luke chapter 6, Jesus said: "No good tree bears bad fruit, nor does a bad tree bear good fruit. Each tree is recognized by its own fruit. People do not pick figs from thornbushes, or grapes from briers. A good man brings good things out of the good stored up in his heart, and an evil man brings evil things out of the evil stored up in his heart. For the mouth speaks what the heart is full of." These teachings emphasize the importance of living a virtuous life and producing good deeds, which are the "fruit" that demonstrate one's true character.

The type of root system in a person's life determines what sort of fruit is produced. Trees produce fruit according to the DNA of the tree. In a similar manner, we bear fruit off of the type of root system at work in our lives. A demonic root system in a person's life can be characterized by a foundation rooted in darkness, sin, and spiritual bondage. This can manifest itself in various ways, such as addiction, pride, anger, bitterness, unforgiveness, and rebellion against God. Such a root system produces bad fruit, which can include negative emotions, destructive behaviors, broken relationships, and a lack of peace and purpose. Ultimately, it leads to spiritual death and separation from God. This is the type of root system that was at work in our lives before we came to Christ. There is the need for healing, deliverance and cleansing to rid ourselves of any ungodly spiritual influences, demonic root systems or ungodly spiritual attachments that may not be fully cut off and destroyed. You can cut down a tree, and the stump can look like it will never grow back. What you see can be deceptive, because even though what's on the surface may look dead, the roots can still be very much alive and continue to grow under the surface. When you need to kill the roots of a large tree, the only way you can do it is by intense heat. The roots must be burned with fire so that they stop growing. In a similar manner, we need to ask Jesus to burn up all the demonic roots in our life with the fire of the

Holy Spirit. It's the fire of God that will destroy all demonic roots in our lives.

On the other hand, a root system established in God is founded on faith, obedience, and a desire to know and love God more deeply. This root system produces good fruit, which can include love, joy, peace, patience, kindness, goodness, faithfulness, gentleness, and self-control. As a person continues to cultivate this root system, they will bear more fruit, and their lives will be characterized by spiritual growth and the expansion of God's kingdom. The Bible uses the analogy of a tree to describe this process. In Psalm 1:3, the person who delights in the law of the Lord is compared to a tree planted by streams of water that yields its fruit in season and whose leaf does not wither.

There are four essential purposes that take place in the root system: nourishment, stability, maturity and expansion. These are a vital part of the health and production of the plant for the purposes of bearing fruit. The Master Gardener has provided a shoot to come forth from the root of Jesse and from His branch will come forth fruit. The Living Bible in 1 Corinthians 3:7 states, "God is important because He is the one who makes things grow." Jesus is the vine; we abide in Him and He abides in us. As branches off of the vine, we are said to be 'in Christ.' Simply put, this means we keep leaning on the Lord, putting our trust in Him, obeying His commands, and maintaining a close relationship with Him. No plant, fruit tree or vine produces fruit the moment it is planted. It is a process that happens over time. It is necessary for the plant to develop a good root system, to draw the nourishment from the roots in order to grow into a strong healthy plant. If you were to take a cutting off of a plant and stick it into dry ground, it would not grow. It would wither and die very quickly. The life of any plant is found in the roots. It is the roots of the plant that enable it to draw the necessary nutrients and moisture from the ground to sustain its life. Subsequently, it is the root system that also enables the plant to grow into maturity and produce fruit.

It is a similar process with Christians. In order to bear good fruit we must allow His words to go down deep in our heart. We must stay in a rich, personal relationship with Christ. He is the source of our strength, and in Him we find life. As He imparts His divine nature to us, we learn to love others through the love of God that is imparted to us. Jesus told His disciples that we are to love one another as He loves all of us, because that is how the world will know we are His disciples. He intends for others, especially unbelievers, to recognize the love of God through good deeds of love and kindness for one another. It is through a meaningful relationship with the Lord that we come to understand the meaning of the scriptures, and use the word of God as our weapon against the enemy. As His words sink deep in our heart, we understand what it means to identify with God as our Father, and the relationship we have as His children. Our identity is with the one who is undefeated, and as His children we have all the rights and privileges that have been afforded to Jesus. We cannot be defeated because He is the king who has triumphed over sin, death and darkness! Anyone who is rooted in the Kingdom of God is unconditionally and without question promised kingdom results. We will have a constant nourishment of revelation knowledge, an immovable, fixed stability, a deep relational fruit bearing maturity, and an ongoing expansive growth to spread throughout the earth.

I had to ask myself some hard questions in reference to my former ministry. Why was it so difficult for me to see kingdom results in my life and ministry? I believed in kingdom principles. I thought my life was hidden in Christ. I believed I was abiding in the vine, but I struggled with little to no fruit coming from the ministry. As I searched for answers, everything came under evaluation and scrutiny. I reviewed my personal habits, relationships, activities, where I was spending my energies, time and talents. Although I could tell that there were some things that were restricting my life, I wasn't sure how to fix the problems. I felt overwhelmed trying to figure it out, and I asked God to take matters out of my hands so that His will would be done. I also didn't find many of the answers I needed until the Lord broke my pot and sent me free. As God brought His intervention to set me free, I saw for the first time that I was root bound. You can't see the roots until they're pulled up and transplanted. It's in the pulling up stage that the spiritual roots were exposed. There were generational curses that were entangled in both the marriage and the ministry that contributed to their failure. Part of my healing was to learn how to work with God for my own self-deliverance. Those things had not been a part of my doctrine or ministry prior to my failure. I tried to fix issues by changing the outward appearance of things, but I wasn't tackling the real problems. God knew there was only one way to get down to the core of the issues, and that was to take His ax to the roots of generational curses and remove demonic attachments.

Pride makes us think we have to keep up the charade. You can put your plant in the sun, fertilize it, and tie a withered, dying plant to a stake to try and make it look better, but those things aren't going to make it healthy. When you look at a root bound plant, the roots that you can't see are the very things that are choking the life out of the plant. I came to realize that there were spiritually rooted things that needed to be cut off, but I also needed to nourish my roots and stabilize my faith. I needed to be transplanted into a place where the soil of my environment had the right conditions for growth and health.

We can slap a new coat of paint on our pot and think it looks good to everyone else. We can even paint the branches of the plant to make them look healthy, but there comes a time when the paint chips off and what's really underneath shows through. The Holy Spirit is the Spirit of Truth. People are walking around with the gifts of the Spirit in them. Why is it we somehow seem to think they're not going to notice if there's something amiss? I got so sick of trying to pretend everything was okay when it wasn't. I hated feeling like a hypocrite. Listen, if you're struggling with living a pretentious, hypocritical life and laying down your pride, just do it. Others can often see what you're trying to hide, so the only person you're really deceiving is yourself. You may try to tell yourself that it's not hurting anyone, but that's not the truth. Living in hypocrisy and not being humble enough to admit you need deliverance and healing is rooted in pride, fear, shame and rejection. Anger and defensiveness will rise up when you feel disrespected or when truth gets too close to home and it will create distance between you and others. Pretending to be someone we are not, or when we are not allowing the Holy Spirit to cultivate good fruit in our life is an indicator that we have not allowed Jesus to be Lord over our emotions and old wounds. It is impossible to overcome an enemy that we refuse to confront in truth. Pride and hypocrisy will break your relationships and leave everyone hurting, resentful, and angry because deep down, they want you to be a person they feel they can respect. Ask God for His help and be willing to accept His solution. The truth is, the enemies of fear, disrespect, disapproval, shame and rejection hold your true identity in captivity until you can admit you've been living in the wrong one. God isn't trying to make you feel better about your old man; He wants the old version of you to die so the new man can come forth, which is the work of Christ in you. Until you fix the root of the problem, you will continue to drain yourself of spiritual effectiveness, emotional and relational health, and the fruit of your life will not be healthy. God will not honor hypocrisy and help you hide it. He loves you enough to expose it, because He wants you to reflect the image of Christ. Hypocrisy robs you of being authentic and finding true love and acceptance; but, honesty and transparency are the path to healing. You have to be willing to face yourself and admit the sin and shame, the pain and dishonor you've experienced that wounded you. So many people, pastors and ministers included, continue to operate out of their old man because they don't want to take the time to let God work in their emotions. God loves us so much that He will put His finger on those things even when we've tried to avoid dealing with them because He wants to heal us. 3 John 2 tells us, "Beloved, I wish that you would prosper in all things and be in health just as your soul prospers." The condition of our soul has a direct relationship with our ability to prosper in other areas of our life, too. It all comes down to what we have believed and the spiritual agreements that we've made, sometimes without realizing it. For instance, if we have a poverty mentality or an orphan spirit, it affects every area of our life and our soul cannot prosper. Neither can our finances. We have to learn where we've agreed with the wrong things and allowed the enemy's assignment to work against us. Then we need to learn how to defeat that poverty mentality by sowing, rehearsing the promises of God, and operating out of faith instead of fear. God wants to deliver us from the things that have us bound so that we can prosper in our soul and every part of our lives.

The Benefits of Deliverance

Deliverance frees people from torment and the influences of evil spirits, and is a powerful tool that can help people find relief from the burdens that weigh them down. By relying on the power of prayer, biblical teachings, and the support of a healthy Christian community, anointed deliverance can provide a path to healing and transformation. For those struggling with addiction or other forms of bondage, Christ centered healing can break the chains that have them bound to certain sins. Deliverance is the removal of demonic attachments, dismantling strongholds and lies, and commanding demonic spirits to leave an individual, which results in a greater level of peace and healing. By addressing the spiritual roots of our issues, we can find the strength and support we need to overcome our struggles. Setting the captives free can have a profound impact on emotional and physical healing and also positively impact other relationships. Here are a few ways that this teaching and ministry can benefit you:

1. Healing from past hurts: Many of us carry wounds from our past that can affect our present relationships. Deliverance can help identify and heal these wounds, freeing us from the negative patterns that can sabotage our relationships and our future opportunities.

2. Breaking generational curses: Our families of origin can also have a powerful impact on our relationships. Deliverance can break generational curses that may be affecting your marriage or relationship, setting you free to build a healthy, thriving partnership.

3. Strengthening spiritual connection: Deliverance can help you deepen your spiritual connection, which can be a powerful source of strength and support in your relationships and to you personally.

4. Building intimacy: As you work through deliverance, you'll deepen your emotional connection to your spouse and build a stronger sense of intimacy. This can help you navigate the ups and downs of life as a team, with a deeper sense of trust and understanding. It also builds intimacy with the Lord. Once the lies have been dealt with and demonic spirits sent away, we are better able to experience a deeper, more intimate connection with the Lord.

Deliverance is a powerful tool to heal and strengthen your walk with God. It releases you from demonic attachments that are there to steal from you. Demonic spirits are assigned to people's lives to weaken them, cause sickness and disease, ruin their relationships and derail their destiny. Deliverance is not a magic solution, but it is a powerful tool that can help put people back in alignment with faith so that God can release restoration in their lives. It has helped countless individuals find healing, hope and transformation. You can identify and address the spiritual roots of your struggles, and build a better future for yourself and your family when you are liberated in Christ. What it comes down to is cooperating with God so that He can remove the things that hinder people's ability to love others better. This also involves learning to love and accept ourselves better, too. If we don't love and accept ourselves, we will have difficulty extending love and acceptance to others. Many people do not have good teaching on deliverance and inner healing available to them, so I would like to recommend two of Laura's books that contain powerful truths, prayers and ministry exercises to help people get down to the root issues of their lives. *Wisdom to Defeat the Enemy* is a deliverance handbook that examines deep issues and contains powerful prayers that cut off demonic attachments. *Holy Spirit, Come Heal Me* is a book that helps foster dialogue and ministry sessions with the Holy Spirit. Both are powerful resources for inner healing and freedom.

Transplanted in the Kingdom

When family and ministry dissolved in California, God graciously gave me a brand new start 2000 miles away in a new state, community, and church that I had no idea even existed. There was a very difficult time before that transition where I felt I could not escape the scrutiny and prying eyes of others. I didn't know that I was going to such a blessed place in a little backwards town just outside of Pensacola. It certainly didn't appear as anything out of the ordinary, and we didn't know anything particularly special about the area. As a matter of fact, it was actually quite a culture shock. It was so different from the big city we were used to. Our eyes were opened to see the wonderful presence of God in the Florida panhandle. It was incredibly fertile ground as far as the movement of the Holy Spirit was concerned. It was an area where God continued to pour out in rich abundance. The churches we were a part of were alive with the ministry of the Holy Spirit and flowing in the spiritual gifts.

God has seen that His children have been rooted in a restrictive mentality and many people's theology is one of confinement. I believe that is why many Christians hope the Lord will come back quickly so that they won't have to deal with more problems in their lifetime. For years, this escapist mentality has been preached from the pulpits and it leads people to believe that the answer is avoidance of the darkness invading the earth. We've been taught that the whole world is going to hell and the answer is to avoid tribulation and wait for the rapture, but this has taught people to be concerned with only themselves. A kingdom mentality is a world vision that is concerned for others and future generations. The church should not be afraid; we serve the King of Kings! We are designed to be the answer to many needs. Our Lord is known as the Lord of Hosts, the Captain of the Angel Armies, and He is on our side.

"Now you are the body of Christ, and each one of you is a part of it. And God has placed in the church first of all apostles, second prophets, third teachers, then miracles, then gifts of healing, of helping, of guidance, and different kinds of tongues. Are all apostles? Are all prophets? Are all teachers? Do all work miracles? Do all have gifts of healing? Do all speak in tongues? Do all interpret? Now eagerly desire the greater gifts." (1 Corinthians 12:27-31).

The gifts are for everyone and should be given room to function in the church so that the church is not weak, compromised and its members left ill equipped for the battles that lie ahead.

"But if all prophesy, and an unbeliever or an ungifted man enters, he is convicted by all, he is called to account by all; the secrets of his heart are disclosed; and so he will fall on his face and worship God, declaring that God is certainly among you," (1 Corinthians 14:24). It is the gift of prophecy that carries with it the power to convict the heart of the unbeliever and bear witness to the power and presence of God. Why then, would anyone want to stifle a gift that has the power and potential to actually grow the church? Why do we seem to fear the gifts will scare people off rather than having faith in the Holy Spirit to draw people to the Lord?

We cannot tell others and tell the Holy Spirit we want God to have His way in our churches if we are not willing to let Him have control of the service. When it comes down to it, many times the message we convey is something like, "God we want you here, but could you try not to make anyone uncomfortable, and could you make sure you don't offend anyone?" As a result, the church has taken on an air of timidity. We should be walking in confidence! Somewhere along the line we've bought into the lies and tactics of the enemy to diminish the effectiveness of the Holy Spirit in exchange for growing the attendance numbers. The result is a church that is severely lacking in spiritual power. It's given us this escapist mentality that is unconcerned about impacting the world around us with the power of God. What about our children and our grandchildren's future? If your son or daughter were enlisted in the military, would you send them to war without training them how to fight? Would you send them to war without giving them any protective gear or weapons? If we don't equip our children with the gifts of the Spirit, we leave them without the very power, authority, and weapons that will ensure their victory over their enemies.

The church must be restored to its full power and authority. The kingdoms of men must come down so that the Kingdom of God can take its rightful place. Doctrines of men, philosophies, tradition, legalism, and religion won't save this world. Only Jesus Christ, who was fully God and fully man, has the power to save mankind. Only Jesus Christ was able to atone for the sin of all mankind and ransomed us from the penalty that our sins deserved. Only Jesus Christ as both God and man can bridge the gap between the two. "Salvation is found in no one else, for there is no other name under heaven given to mankind by which we must be saved." (Acts 4:12). If for no other reason than this, we should at the very least make a commitment to come into relationship with the one who paid the ultimate price with His life, because Jesus gave us the opportunity to know Him on a personal level. Religion divides, keeps people in individual pots, and places constraints on a person's heart and life. Religion will always limit one's faith and ability to grow in Christ. A relationship with God is very different. A relationship with Christ promotes love, compassion, forgiveness, and unity. Christ and His Holy Spirit will always, always encourage you to grow and keep growing. In the Kingdom of God there are no limits to how much a person can grow or accomplish. God works with unrealized potential and limitless possibilities in every person. We are only limited by our level of faith and what we believe is possible. Laura heard the Lord tell her one day, "Never let anyone quantify you." In other words, He was telling her not to let another person define her by their assessment of what they thought she should be or what they thought she was capable of. We should all be careful that we don't let others determine our potential. No one other than God himself can assess our worth or the possibilities of what we can accomplish with His power activated in our life. All things are possible to those that believe! So, never let someone else appraise your value or rate your capability

72

based on how they see you, because they have absolutely no idea what God has planned for your future. Take the labels and the limits off! This should give us confidence to draw near to God and walk in love towards others. When the walls of separation in the body of Christ come down, it brings unity and the anointed flow of God's Holy Spirit. Where the Holy Spirit is, there is power. Jesus never intended us to preach a watered down gospel, restrict the movement of the Holy Spirit, or walk around intimidated by the enemy.

It is time that we each walk in confidence, knowing that God is for us, not against us. Darkness will increase upon the Earth but we have the light of Christ within us; that light will never go out as long as we continue in our relationship with Him. We are to be light and truth in the midst of the darkness, and a voice crying in the wilderness, "Prepare the way for the Lord!" My Bible says that the path of the just is as a shining light that shines more and more unto that coming day. We have been translated into a Kingdom of Light. Light repels darkness, and we are to go and push back evil. My Bible says that God has made us to be a kingdom of priests and we shall reign on the earth. My Bible says that the kingdoms of this world have become the kingdom of our Lord and of His Christ, and He will reign forever and ever. My Bible says that now has come the salvation and the authority of His Christ. There are thousands of verses and promises for the people of God who are rooted in His kingdom. The enemy who was defeated at Calvary is still a defeated foe! He is not more powerful than our Lord. I refuse to believe the lies of the enemy. By the grace of God, Satan will not claim my children, my health, my finances, or my future. I don't want to forfeit one promise that God says is mine. Never, never, never give in. Never surrender your faith. Never surrender your confidence towards God.

We are conquerors through Him who loves us! We are not to retreat in fear, but to March forward in victory. We are not those that shrink back from a challenge and we do not entertain an escapist mentality. In order to advance the cause of Christ and increase the influence of the kingdom of God on the earth, we must take responsibility for things that place limits upon our faith. We must break out of our restricted way of thinking and enlarge our hearts for a world harvest.

The Apostle Paul tells the believer to be rooted and built up in Christ. This means we must be centered on God's everlasting, triumphant kingdom. We have been given the keys to this kingdom. Our commission has been made clear in scripture. Daniel 7:27 says, "...then the sovereignty, power and greatness of the kingdoms under the whole heaven will be handed over to the saints, the people of the most high. His kingdom will be an everlasting kingdom and all rulers will worship and obey Him." Our first charge from the Father, found in the book of Genesis, is to be fruitful and increase in number. Fill the earth and subdue it, and rule over creation. The Lord Jesus has given us all authority to overcome all the power of the enemy. The Holy Spirit has empowered us to evict demons and subject every demonic principality and power to the Lord's headship. Joshua carried out the commands of the Lord. They had defeated and conquered the inhabitants of Canaan. The country was brought under the control of the Israelites. They subdued the land. God went before them and hardened the hearts of their enemies. No one wanted to be subjected to the Israelites. The Gibeonites were the only exception. We are complete in Christ when we have Him; we're filled with God when we have Christ. He is the highest ruler, with authority over every other power. "So, you also are complete through your union with Christ, who is the head over every ruler and authority." (Colossians 2:10, NLT) The enemy was stripped of his power and authority at the cross. When we accept Christ as our Savior, we die to our old nature and rise again as a new creation. We are the seat of His authority, and His kingdom people; we take dominion everywhere we step.

God establishes us in our Promised Land when we take a foothold in what the enemy has claimed for himself. He will take as much as he can get until we put our foot down and say, no more! We are to subdue our enemies and take dominion over the earth. Stepping in faith to believe for your promised land is only made possible by the experiential knowledge of God's love. His forgiveness and mercy are simply unfathomable. Jesus was belittled, mocked, spit upon, rejected, accused, put to shame, beaten and crucified by the very people that He came to save. He had done nothing wrong at all and was completely innocent of all charges brought against Him. In our humanity, we cannot even imagine another person enduring this sort of thing for us, much less for people that despised Him. God's love knows no bounds. It cannot be measured. He is not like us, and He doesn't withhold His love when we do something wrong. God, in His everlasting mercy, forgave us when Jesus died in our place on the cross. He bridged the gap between man and God. Our Father has done everything possible for us to live in relationship with Him; all we have to do is say yes.

It is this amazing revelation of God's love that assures us we are accepted in Christ. This is what gives us confident assurance that His love for us is unshakable and He is fully invested to help us fulfill our destiny. This good news is also the message of hope we share with others. When we see others struggling in their own personal battles or lost because they don't know the good news is for them, we share the message of hope that we have found through Christ our Savior. This brings expansion and growth to the Kingdom of God, and we become rooted in our land.

The stories of conquest in the Old Testament show us that God had no tolerance for sin or enemies that were set on the destruction of His people. Many of these stories can be seen as testimonies of deliverance. He told His people not to be soft or let any enemy remain alive; to do so would be a big mistake because they could rise up at a later date to come after them again. It is the same with evil spirits. We cannot afford to compromise with them or make excuses to justify sin in our lives, or it will continue to be a problem that plagues us and our family. Demonic spirits look for opportunities to gain access in our lives through areas of our life where we are careless. They look for things they can exploit that we fail to pray about. They tempt us to make agreements with them so they have legal grounds to remain in our lives. Demons look for places where they have been invited in. You might think, "I wouldn't do that," but demons see opportunity through our negligence. Generational iniquity, which are sins that our ancestors opened a door to but never repented for their sins, is a huge blind spot for many people. Demons have access to their lives that they are unaware of and those things continue to affect a person's ability to live in freedom, health and victory. Generational curses show up in families because children learn to repeat habits, behaviors and attitudes from parents, grandparents and other ancestors. If those behaviors are in disobedience to God's word, demons see opportunity to form assignments, reproducing those same sins in future generations. Repentance, confession, renouncement and obedience cut off demonic attachments and close the door so that the enemy cannot continue to harass us or enforce a curse.

There is only one thing that God is relentless to destroy, and that is demonic spirits. God never shows mercy to demons. He will bring judgment upon the enemy because His love compels Him to set His people free. We must learn to see things from the perspective that it's His **love** that comes to uproot the enemies in our life. He doesn't withhold His goodness just to penalize us. That's not His heart or His character, but it is a lie the enemy will use to make you think that God is difficult to please and living a Christian life is not worth the trouble. He wants us to go to war against the lies that rage against and resist God's truth. He wants us to ask the right questions so that He can help us gain the victory! There are several ways in which people can misunderstand God's intentions when they are going through spiritual battles. Here are a few:

1. Blaming God: When people go through difficult times, they may blame God for their struggles. They may see their problems as punishment from God, when in reality, God is trying to wake them up, expose where the enemy is active in their life, and set them free from spiritual bondage. The spiritual warfare can lead to a misunderstanding of God's intentions and cause people to turn away from Him. The orphan spirit will scream rebellious, accusing thoughts towards God and try to turn your heart away from the Father that loves you. It will tell you that God has abandoned you and doesn't love you, otherwise you wouldn't be going through certain painful situations. A religious spirit will tell you that you aren't doing enough, you're in sin, or you don't qualify for a blessing, whatever brings you back under condemnation. It is always the enemy that tries to turn our hearts away from God so that we will form an agreement with him. God cannot bless what is in agreement with the enemy's ways, such as rebellion, accusation, or unbelief.

2. Lack of Understanding: Sometimes people lack understanding about spiritual warfare and the role it plays in our lives. There are two sides to warfare. One side is what the enemy is doing to cause confusion, suffering, and destruction. On the other side is what God is doing to bring the person into greater revelation, increase their discernment and expose spiritual darkness. They may not recognize that the battles they face are intended to set them free from demonic attachments and influences and bring them into greater victory. If a person doesn't learn how to war effectively, it can lead to confusion and a lack of faith in God's plan. The enemy always wants to lead us in our thoughts to a place of fear, anxiety and stress. God wants to bring us into a place of rest. Take the time to pray, worship, and rest in God's presence. Ask Him, "What do you want me to learn from this? What do you want to be for me right now in these circumstances?" For example, if your need is finances, God wants you to realize He is your source of provision. If your confidence is in the wrong things, he will sometimes allow those things to be removed so that you must look to Him. When He supplies what you lack, that is how He builds trust. He shows you that He is dependable to provide for your needs. If you need healing, ask God to show you the revelation that may be preventing your healing from coming forth. Sometimes we have unknowingly made an agreement with a wrong attitude or a wrong spirit that is blocking us from receiving the goodness of God. Perhaps He requires a step of faith and obedience to unlock His blessing and answer to your prayers. Whatever it is we lack is often the very thing that God wants to become for us during times of spiritual warfare. When you enter a place of rest, you are better able to hear from God.

3. Resistance to Change: People may resist the changes that God is trying to bring about in their lives through spiritual battles. They may be comfortable in their current circumstances and not want to let go of the things that are holding them back. Why is it that we seem to embrace the things that are not good for us and keep us stuck, unhealthy, spiritually weak or broken? We need to ask ourselves what benefit we receive from resisting change. What thoughts are magnifying fear? Fear and unbelief are just as much sin as persisting in some negative habit, because the

Bible says that whatever is not of faith is sin. Fear, unbelief, or areas of sin that we can't seem to overcome are an indication of strongholds in the belief system and demonic attachments in a person's life. They are there to prevent us from receiving God's best and allowing the thief and destroyer to continue to have access to us and our family. Is it really worth it? It is never a good thing to prefer darkness over light, or sin and a life of compromise over purity and a right relationship with God. "Whoever conceals their sins does not prosper, but the one who confesses and renounces them finds mercy." (Proverbs 28:13)

4. Focusing on the Wrong Things: Sometimes people focus too much on the negative aspects of their spiritual battles and not enough on the positive outcome that God has in store for them. They may become discouraged and lose sight of the fact that God's love compels Him to set them free from sin, generational curses, and demonic influences. When the enemy is trying to bring confusion, discouragement or turn your heart away from God, speak His promises out loud. Faith comes by hearing the word of God. Rehearse the goodness of God and take time to remember the times He has come through for you. Remind the enemy of those times! Look up testimonies of how He showed up for others. Don't allow the father of lies to bring further discouragement and magnify unbelief. It takes faith to please God. God does not bless unbelief or fear. He responds to faith. Keep focused on His goodness and His heart of love towards you, and declare faith into the atmosphere. Bind demonic spirits of heaviness and oppression. Loose the Spirit of Truth, Peace and Joy. Worship to break the spirits set against your peace. Prophecy His word until you get to the other side of your trial.God will bring you to the other side.

To avoid these misunderstandings, it's important to seek God's wisdom and guidance during spiritual battles. Reading the Bible, praying, and seeking counsel from trusted spiritual leaders can help us gain a better understanding of God's intentions and the role that spiritual warfare plays in our lives. We must trust that God has our best interests at heart and that He wants to set us free so that we can live the abundant life that He has planned for us. God helped His people defeat their enemies, and when others tried to curse them, He turned it into a blessing. God wouldn't allow others to curse what He had not cursed. He always watched over his people to ensure their success! Their response was to believe in His promises and act in obedience to His word, and He helped them overcome every adversary that stood against them. When it was all over and the battles had been won, the Israelites possessed the land and it was time to enjoy the victory. A very grateful Joshua renewed his covenant of love and commitment to God, as well as a challenge to his brethren with these words: "Choose you this day whom you will serve, but as for me and my house we will serve the Lord." (Joshua 24:15) This great leader rededicated himself and his house to the living God. This is the stand we take when the enemy wants to undermine our resolve to place our trust in God.

Essential Purpose # 1 - Nourishment

In the beginning of the chapter, we mentioned the four purposes of the root system. Nourishment is one of the most vital. The Apostle Paul prayed that the church would be rooted in love. We have wonderful, powerful examples of faith filled Christians listed in Hebrews 11, but our faith also needs the nourishment of God's unconditional love. Laura and I were overwhelmed by the Lord's demonstration of love and forgiveness. Failure can be devastating. I had failed in so many ways and the enemy tried to convince me that I would never minister again.

Satan worked overtime to convince me that God would never speak to me or answer my prayers. One person who I had offended wrote to me to tell me that God would not hear me and that the heavens would always be like brass. This person wanted me to feel as though God had rejected me. During that period of time I received a lot of discouraging words from people who only thought they knew what God was thinking. They erred by placing their emotions and offenses higher than God's mercy, and in their conclusion they decided their opinions were God's judgment towards me. In reality, it was nothing more than offended people with a religious spirit. They believed God was harsh and punishing and projected that on to others. It seemed that the more people went out of their way to send us word curses, the more God went out of His way to bless us. As I ran to my Father in repentance, He ran to me with outstretched arms, assuring me of His love. Psalm 46:1 became a word of faith to feed on. "The Lord is my refuge and strength, and ever present help in times of trouble."

Isaiah 42:3 is a prophecy about the servant of God (Jesus) that reveals the compassionate heart of God to those that are hurting and broken. "A bruised reed He will not break, and a smoldering wick He will not snuff out. In faithfulness He will bring forth justice." The metaphor of a bruised reed refers to a person who is weak, vulnerable, or injured in some way, while the smoldering wick refers to a person who is on the verge of giving up or losing hope. The verse is saying that the Lord would be gentle and compassionate towards such people, rather than harsh or cruel. Those that speak from offense, spite or an unloving attitude don't know the heart of God towards His people. Although He is not soft on sin, He also is not cruel. He understands the lies, trickery and temptations that come from the enemy because He was also tempted, and He has compassion on us in our weaknesses. His love and comfort are always available.

God came down and visited me and my wife. He whispered His words of encouragement in our ears. He brought His mercy, forgiveness, and grace and He never left us. He was in fact the one who had orchestrated our deliverance and brought us to a city of refuge. We fed on everything that magnified His love and mercy. God told us to humble ourselves and show forgiveness and mercy to others, especially those that had rejected us. There is an incredible blessing of freedom and love that takes place when you bless those that position themselves against you as an enemy. Our hearts were born again with a powerful passion and understanding of God's grace. It's with that love that we offer ourselves to Him. "Therefore, in view of God's mercy, offer up your bodies as a living sacrifice." (Romans 12:1).

His love compels us and leads us toward the destiny of our dreams. Our prayers become an affirmation of what He has already given us. Instead of my wife and I praying wishful prayers, hoping we might be able to be worthy of entering our promises, we began calling those things that are not as if they were, being fully persuaded that God had power to do what He had promised. Faith became activated from a worshiping, grateful heart to a heart bold with passion, power and warfare. In prayer and fasting we began to tear down every giant, every wall, and move every obstacle that stood in the path of His promises. From finances and ministry to the salvation of our own children, we declared the promises of God. We posted scriptures throughout our apartment, believing in breakthroughs.

The testimony God gave us of healing, salvation, and ongoing answers for provision added a greater appetite for our walk of faith. We were no longer satisfied with any other lifestyle. The mundane, former way of living brought no satisfaction to our spiritual palate. Anything else tastes very bland compared to a faith-filled diet. In Numbers 14:9,

Caleb declared that the giants of the land would be food for them. Caleb had a taste for a giant-eater diet. Once a person has consumed a few giants, they just can't go back to milk and cookies.

Essential Purpose #2 - Stability

Stability is the second function of the root system. It becomes a foundation for the massive trunk and branches that extend with foliage and fruit. A solid root system will cause trees to weather a tremendous amount of pressure from storms and wind. Jesus gave the example of the wise man that built his house upon the rock. It stood against a great storm because it had its foundation built on the rock. Jesus started this parable by saying that the man who heard the word and obeyed it would find security. I have talked with many other leaders about their plans for securing their future. Like everyone else, pastors are concerned with retirement plans, property investments, living wills and financial portfolios. Although there is wisdom in planning your financial security, many leaders will avoid certain risky decisions that place their retirement at risk. Stability and security in the kingdom is predicated on hearing and doing the will of God.

We also judge spiritual stability and others by longevity and consistency. Family ties, marriages, memberships, employment and community roots become the measuring rod for a faithful person. It's not that any of these things are wrong, it's just that none of those things actually require faith. The word faithful means to be filled with, or full of faith. A faithful person is a Christian who is full of faith. God entrusts the responsibility in stewardship of the kingdom of God to risk takers. True faith requires taking risks and stepping out in faith. Those who were chosen in Acts 6:1 were men full of the Holy Spirit and wisdom. Steven and Philip were examples of putting their stability and security on the line. Those who were given talents and commended by the Master were risk takers. I believe in the institutions that God has given us. Country, community, family and church have been and will continue to be a bedrock for our society. God also said that everything that can be shaken will be shaken. That which cannot be shaken will remain. (Hebrews 12:26-27).

Every time we uproot the enemy's lies, his influence, and cut away at the tangled root system the enemy has formed in our belief system, the healthy root system of the Lord can get a better grip into the soil of His kingdom. Our roots go down deeper into the assurance of God's love, and we become anchored in the hope we have in Christ. Our ability to trust Him in all things becomes stronger and more confident. Our roots go down deeper with each trial that we overcome, and our stability increases because *we know Him*. We understand His ways. The storms of life will not move us.

We have heard messages about restructuring, a shift, and God doing a new thing for many years. While the church will always be around, the way we understand the form will change. We, the people, are the church. We have the spirit of God. It's not the local church, although we all need the benefit of the faith community. The current model of church as we have known it must change, and it will. The church, or shall we say, the body of Christ acting as the church, must pour themselves out into their communities, get into the streets, and take Christ to others. It's not about getting people into a building; it's about introducing Jesus to them so that Christ can get into them. God wants to expand His kingdom, not just build bigger buildings. The net is too small to hold the great catch of fish the Lord is bringing in. These are a few of the changes that mark the difference between the church age and the kingdom age. When God shakes, He brings trials and testing. He tests us to see where our loyalties are, but the enemy wants to know, too. This is a time when God will ask us to lay our Isaac on the altar and surrender it all. Trials by fire determine whether what people have built is works of the flesh, or if they have eternal value in the kingdom. There are good people that cannot tell the difference between building God's kingdom and building their own. God may just unravel everything and let all their good efforts fail. When transition hits, things that once worked in the last season often won't get the same results in the new season. Sometimes the thing we've been doing is simply no longer needed because it has run its course and God has something better in mind. We don't always understand that though, and we must resist discouragement or a desire to hold on to what God is asking people to release.

Failure and deep discouragement are the ultimate test of the heart. Changes of this sort have the potential to overwhelm many into depression, despair, and hopelessness. There will be ministry leaders that will have to look for a different type of work rather than place their expectation on others to support them. These changes must come in order to make room for God's kingdom on earth. Those that are afraid of change, individuals that get a sense of identity or self-worth from their works, and those that are in it for selfish gain may experience a sense of fear and despair when everything comes unraveled. Fear of change can cause both the message and God's messengers to be rejected, because others are afraid of it being a true message from God. Fear will cause people to be suspicious and accusing, and question the motives of others. It can also make people react with anger and defensiveness. We must recognize at this moment the entire world is in a major transition. Messengers of reformation are often persecuted because of those that are unwilling to adapt to change. These are the people that are often controlled by fear and religious spirits. This is both a warning of what is to come as well as a call to intercession.

Transitions often require us to step outside of our comfort zones and face new challenges. This can lead to personal growth and development as we learn new skills, gain new experiences, and become more resilient. Transitions can also prompt us to reflect on our values, beliefs, and goals. This can help us become more self-aware and better understand what we want out of life. We are forced to adapt to new circumstances and situations. This can improve our ability to cope with change and become more adaptable in the future. Transitions can open up new opportunities for us to try new things and have new experiences. This can be exciting and enriching, and can help us broaden our horizons. Successfully navigating a transition can also boost our confidence and self-esteem, as we prove to ourselves that we are capable of overcoming challenges and achieving our goals. Overall, while transitions can be difficult and challenging, they can also bring significant personal growth and development.

There is room to grow and be fruitful in the kingdom, where there is no need to feel confined or competitive with others. At times, it can be quite difficult to feel like we have found the right place where we fit, especially if our focus is finding it in a specific local church. However, in the kingdom of God, there is room for everyone to find where they fit in anointed service. It is a place where we are valued, accepted and our gifts and abilities find their right expression to bless others in our community. Some may or may not agree, but I believe the church must return to a kingdom model of fruitfulness as it is displayed in the Book of Acts. The body of Christ must be emptied out into our cities and communities. Many ministry leaders will feel threatened by that thought because they may feel their livelihood is at risk. Don't give in to panic. Many are about to enter a time of completely trusting God. They haven't walked this way before, but it's okay. God is trustworthy, and He has people that have already gone through these sorts of changes and transitions. They have gone through the fires of adversity, loneliness, fear of financial loss, and worked through trust issues with the Lord. They have the testimonies to prove it. The church as we've known it must change in order to make room for people to be planted and become fruitful in the Kingdom of God. God has called and arranged for a change of garments in this new season. He has new mantles and new assignments to help people get through times of transition. Ministry will take many different forms in the days ahead, and many of these changes will come swiftly. The paradigm shifts we started hearing about a couple of decades ago are upon us. The Lord has leaders that are ready to help comfort, guide and encourage those that are walking in unfamiliar territory so that they do not have to feel alone and afraid. This is a time to ask the Lord for clarity, divine connections and strategy. As we lean on Him, we will once again discover his unwavering faithfulness and grace to navigate through troubled waters.

What will save our country from moral decline and depravity will not be patriotism, family values, the Ten Commandments or even prayer in schools. It will be the voice of faith-filled, spirit led, kingdom rooted believers who are willing to risk reputation, security, and stability to advance the Gospel of Jesus Christ.

Leaving what we have associated as our source of provision, safety and identity is a difficult process that involves breaking away from something that you may hold dear to your heart, and while you endeavor to walk into the unknown, it can be like grieving the loss of someone very dear to you. It's almost like you don't know who you are without that particular thing in your life. It's ok if you feel lost. God knows right where you are and He is right beside you. This journey is secured by walking in oneness, not only with your spouse if you have one, but to be one with His Spirit. Ecclesiastes 4:9 tells us that two are better than one because they have a good return for their work. One may be overpowered, but two can defend themselves. When a person takes risks for the kingdom it is necessary to be 100% certain of His presence in your life. We need to be able to say, "Lord, we cannot go anywhere or accomplish anything without your presence." I'm so grateful for my wife. She is my friend, encouragement, and spiritual partner. She is also my Deborah, my Esther, my Ruth, and my Mary. She is my battle ax in times of spiritual warfare, my shield and comfort in times of turmoil. We have experienced a great deal together. We walk, breathe, and live as one because we have risked it all and allowed the Holy Spirit to bind us together like the threefold strand that cannot be easily broken. We are rooted in His kingdom.

Essential Purpose #3 - Maturity

The third function of the root system is maturity. A plant can only produce in direct proportion to the growth of its root system. The deeper the roots, the bigger the tree; the bigger the tree, the greater shade and fruit bearing it becomes. In Matthew 13:31, Jesus compared a mustard seed to the Kingdom of God. Although it is the smallest of all the seeds, when it is planted in His field, it grows and becomes the largest of all the plants. Eventually, it becomes a tree and the birds of the air come and perch in its branches. God is in the growing business. In Hebrews 6:1, the Apostle Paul urges his readers to grow in their understanding and knowledge of the Christian faith, and to not remain stuck in a state of spiritual immaturity. He lists a few of the "elementary teachings" that he believes his readers should already be familiar with, including repentance from acts that lead to death and faith in God. By saying "not laying again the foundation," Paul is essentially saying that these truths should be so ingrained in his readers that they do not need to be re-taught or revisited.

Gifts were given to the church that we would build up and become mature attaining to the whole measure of the fullness of Christ. There is nothing that can mature a person quicker than the steps of faith that are tested by the trials of life. These trials, tests, and His methods of discipline are the way God imparts His nature to us. More of His nature is imparted to us every time we allow love to express itself through our faith filled actions.

Essential Purpose #4 - Expansion

The final purpose of the root system is expansion. The sign of a maturing plant is evident by its growth. The roots continue to grow and spread out, enabling the plant to thrive. If you have ever had a tree in your yard that starts to have its roots invade your plumbing, then you know the strength and tenacity of the growth of that root system. If it is not controlled it will break the foundation of the house, the driveway and anything else that gets in the way. Roots are naturally relentless in expanding their territory. The tree will go through great lengths to tap into any water source or source of nutrition available. The base and trunk of that tree begins to enlarge itself as the roots provide more and more space for growth. When the root system is healthy, the plant will naturally produce good fruit. Our Father is constantly examining our lives for fruit. He wants us to bear good fruit and fill the earth. Sometimes that means He prunes, or cuts off things we have been doing or relationships that will hinder our growth. The pruning process cuts, and it often hurts. Give the hurt and disappointments to God and be careful not to harbor offense. There will be a new season with new relationships and activities. The Lord wants us to reach out and pursue all His good promises until every last one of them is fulfilled. We attain to the full measure of Christ, having confidence that what he has begun in us He will complete and perform. Christians also have a God-given spiritual desire to enlarge ourselves. It began at the garden where we were told to replenish the earth, and it is reiterated in the gospels as we are instructed to go into all the world. The Holy Spirit provokes that dream into a global mission of peace.

This gospel is a gospel of peace. It is meant to grow and expand to all the nations. The God of hope fills you with all joy and peace as you trust in Him, that you may overflow with hope by the power of the Holy Spirit. That gospel that overflows with joy, peace, and righteousness compels us to bring breakthrough to others. It is our hope and strength. "The God of peace will soon crush Satan under your feet," (Romans 16:20). The spreading of this kingdom is not followed by sounds of serenity but the sound of crushing demons under our feet. Our peace is Satan's torment.

We have gone to many homes and visited many families with the good news of Jesus Christ. We teach people how to break curses and get free. There is an importance to share the gospel publicly, but also house to house. It is how the early church grew so rapidly. The apostles reached whole regions in a couple of years. The early disciples were so effective at filling the world with the good news of the kingdom that it was said of them in Acts 17:6, "that they had caused trouble all over the world." God continues to fill the earth with His glory. The exciting thing is, the best is yet to come! We give praise to the one who does exceedingly, immeasurably more than what we ask or think.

There are many places in scripture where people are compared to trees. Psalm 1 compares and contrasts the wicked and the righteous. The blessing is upon the righteous who do not give themselves to the same activities as the wicked. It is the person that takes delight in God's word that discovers His blessing. "That person is like a tree planted by streams of water which yields its fruit in season, and whose leaf does not wither. Whatever they do prospers." (Psalm 1:3). Ezekiel 47 also uses imagery that speaks of a tree planted by a river. The tree's leaves are for healing, and its fruit is for food. The healing leaves of the tree represent spiritual healing and the restorative power of God's grace and mercy. The fruit of the tree represents the spiritual nourishment that comes from a close relationship with God. The analogy of the tree planted by the river that becomes healing for the nations is ultimately a message of hope and restoration. It reminds us that God's presence and provision can bring healing and nourishment to all who seek Him, and that His blessings are available to all who trust in Him. Without a doubt, praise and worship with a grateful heart is what releases the power of God to flow in and through your life. Never underestimate the power of thanksgiving, praise and worship. It draws the Lord closer, releases revelation, and invites angelic activity where you need assistance. When the river of God flows through you, the power and presence of God will increase in your life and expand your reach to touch more people. God will grow your influence and take your life's message to more and more people as you trust Him to expand your ministry.

Prayer for Growth and Stability

Dear Heavenly Father,

Open the eyes of my heart and give me the understanding that will help me grow into all that You have for me and my family. Help me to let go of all the things that are not good for me and hold fast to the things that will be healing for my soul. Give me eyes to see you clearly and accurately so that I don't misunderstand who you are or misunderstand your motives. Above all, help me practice gratitude every day.

Holy Spirit, take the fire of God to burn up every demonic root system in my life. Pull up every bit of root system that is unhealthy and plant something good and godly in its place. Uproot the lies of the enemy and replace it with truth. If I have agreed with lies, show me and I will repent. Lead me into greater healing and freedom.

Let the river of God flow within me. Help me shift my focus off my questions, my wants and needs onto simply praising you with a grateful heart. May Your Holy Spirit adjust my heart posture so that I please You with my worship and my conversations. Please let praise break me free in any area where I have been bound. Let praise open up new portals that bring heavenly revelation. Lord, I pray that my life honors you. Please give me creative ideas on how to increase my ability to touch others with the good news about you, Jesus. Help me show others how to get free and live a victorious life in Christ. Increase my influence and my ability to reach more people with the message of hope and healing. I pray that my testimonies reach the people you want to help.

Father, anchor my hope in the truth of your word and in the character and integrity of Christ as a person. I pray that you would bring me to maturity and help me grow into a tree of righteousness. In Jesus' name, amen.

ROOM TO GROW

CHAPTER SIX
CHURCH PLANTED VS. KINGDOM PLANTED

The type of environment that we are in has a direct effect on our personal growth and our worldview. We tend to fear what is unknown about the future, but this can create a fear of change. Negative self-talk and self-doubt causes us to doubt our abilities or evaluate ourselves based on our own internal measuring rod that determines our sense of worthiness to obtain success. Uncomfortable feelings such as anxiety or worry can become behaviors that are rooted in self-sabotage if a person allows the voice of fear to persuade them to avoid that discomfort. We must come to realize that growth and change involve taking risks. It is natural to experience fear of failure, embarrassment or shame at the thought of things not working out, but aversion to discomfort, playing it safe, and avoiding steps of faith are the surest way to come face to face with the failure we were hoping to avoid. Failure should be a learning process. We will all experience failure at *something*, but it's what we do with that experience that determines our future. Don't let fear and doubt cripple your future. Our minds want us to play it safe because we feel more at peace when things are predictable and familiar, but our Spirit wants to live large and experience what life is like in uncharted waters. God wants to lead us into risk taking adventures so that He can show us what He is capable of as Christ lives through us.

Planted in a Pot vs. Planted in an Open Field

Transplanting is a design of God that allows for growth, productivity and fruitfulness. We may not like the challenges, but God designs the journey. If we desire to fulfill the dream God has for us, there is a necessity to let go of the old way of thinking and the old wineskin. You have to recognize the enemies of indecision and procrastination that stop you from making important decisions. If you are asking the Lord to enable you to bear more fruit, if you desire the new wine and you're crying out for revival, you must prepare yourself for the continual adjusting and shaking off of the old, familiar way of life. There are some differences between being planted in the church vs. being planted in the Kingdom of God. I have listed some of them. This is not meant to be a criticism of the church. I believe in the local church and its function; however, I believe the church is in transition to birth sons and daughters into the kingdom.

In a church or religious environment, there is the expectation of conformity to an established tradition, way of living or a set of beliefs. People are generally a bit uncomfortable with others that challenge the status quo. There's a well known little phrase that says, *"When in Rome, do as the Romans do,"* which implies the importance of conforming to the customs, traditions or behaviors of others when you are in their presence or in a certain place. The message is, "Don't rock the boat." If you're in a place where there is no freedom to do things differently, where others discourage your desire to take new steps, or you find there is no room for growth, then you are planted in a pot where your faith is restricted. You may even be criticized for wanting more for your life.

On the other hand, if you are planted in an environment where there are no restrictions on your creativity, faith, and imagination, there are no limitations to your potential. We all face challenges and setbacks, but God builds leaders by teaching them to persevere and overcome obstacles. We must learn to have a strong sense of determination to thrive and not settle for mere survival. We can not be easily deterred by failure. Failure is an opportunity to learn, but it doesn't mean we are failures. God wants to transform our mindset. He wants to bless us with the inspired creativity of God and give us innovative ideas for expansion. People with a growth mindset are open to new ideas and perspectives. The open field of God's kingdom is to be in an environment that fosters passion and visionary thinking so that it can be communicated clearly.

Needs Driven vs. Purpose Driven

People that are driven by their needs are generally focused on meeting their immediate needs for food, shelter, safety and social belonging. They are driven by immediate gratification of pressing needs. Sometimes those needs are emotional. People that feel isolated, lonely or emotionally needy may try to press others to meet those needs for friendship, acceptance, and validation. Many people seek the assistance of a local church for those very reasons. There is a tremendous amount of fear, anxiety and stress when we lack the necessities of life. Laura and I experienced that, too. God puts us in miracle-needing circumstances so that He can enlarge our faith for the miraculous. There is so much shame and a feeling of humiliation when we cannot provide our basic needs for ourselves or our families, but God wants us to feel and experience what others have gone through, too. He takes us through hard places to work humility into our character, to learn to appreciate the struggles others experience without judging them, and to develop gratitude, but He also stretches our faith so that we put a demand on the anointing and pull out miracles. God wants us to have answers for others to help them navigate their own times of transition. When we have pressing concerns over immediate essential needs, our soul is not at rest and it makes it difficult to focus and hear from God. We also noticed it was very obvious among the homeless, the addicted, those that were in various sorts of bondage and in need of deliverance. They are very restless. Demons don't allow people to come into God's rest. They bring torment and their presence results in chaos. If we learn to minister first to a person's needs, then their soul will quiet down and be more at rest so that we can make disciples.

In contrast, those who are driven by a sense of purpose experience a fulfillment and joy that comes from contributing to a higher purpose, or something greater than themselves. They are often willing to sacrifice their immediate needs for long term goals. People that are led by a sense of purpose tend to be more focused and intentional in prioritizing their time to achieve their goals. When people pursue opportunities to help others in their community, they gain a sense of direction. What are you good at? Is there something in your skill set that people are willing to pay for? The questions people have asked of God such as, "Why am I here?" or, "What is my purpose in life?" unlocks something powerfully satisfying within them when they do what they are created to do.

Meeting Oriented vs. Presence Oriented

People attend church meetings for a variety of reasons. Some people feel an obligation or a sense of duty, or perhaps they have other motivations, such as socializing or networking. I was a pastor's son, so I was practically raised in church and attended church with my family every time the church was open. Then I went to Bible College and married a pastor's daughter at the age of 19, so my entire life was spent attending and serving the church. It was not optional. People may attend meetings for some of the same reasons, because of the expectations of others and a sense of obligation. Church attendance may also be viewed as something people do to pacify others and keep the peace in the household, but it doesn't mean that their attendance is because they are pursuing the presence of God.

Someone that is driven by the pursuit of God's presence is passionate for the Lord and is looking for a deeper connection with Him. Their intentions for showing up are different. They want to *experience* Him and be touched in their emotions. Often they are looking for healing, revelation, impartation or awakening. Their motivation comes from the heart, rather than simply attending a meeting out of habit or obligation.

Heaven is the Goal vs. Heaven on Earth

Jesus taught the doctrine known as "the Kingdom of God." There are many passages where Jesus spoke on the Kingdom of God. One example is the Lord's Prayer found in Matthew 6:9-13, where Jesus taught His disciples to pray that the Kingdom of God would come on earth as it is in heaven. We are called to influence the culture and release the Kingdom of God through the preaching of the gospel and demonstrating the power of God. We are not called to run from the challenge.

An escapist mentality is unbiblical. There are many messages that might appeal to those that simply want to enjoy a comfortable, prosperous, easygoing ministry, but the Bible does not emphasize those things as a measuring rod for success. The Apostle Paul was not under any such delusion. He understood full well that there was a price to pay for advancing the gospel, and that faithfulness to God brings difficulty, but he didn't seek to escape adversity prematurely. God needed him alive to complete his mission on earth. Paul boasted in the Lord for the things he endured, but his constant concern was for the state of the churches. His love for others as their spiritual father compelled him to do everything within his power to make sure they were growing in truth and developing good fruit. His challenge to the early church is the same today. Examine yourselves as to whether you are in the faith. "For the Spirit God has not given us does not make us timid, but gives us power, love, and self discipline." (2 Timothy 1:7)

Church Policy Led vs. Spirit Led

Churches that are led by policies and traditions typically have a church board and appointed leaders. There is nothing wrong with this, unless those making the decisions restricts the life and flow of the Holy Spirit. Many times the emphasis is on budgets, programs, and the politics of church life, rather than seeking revelation and direction from the Lord. Sometimes there are personal agendas and impure motives that get in the way of making the best decisions, and the preference of the Holy Spirit is either not sought or ignored. It is important to the life of the church that the people in various positions are there because God has appointed them where to serve. Many churches forfeit the anointing because they have the wrong people in places of service and they aren't anointed or have the maturity to do that job. Just because someone can, doesn't mean they are the person God would choose. When people are simply filling a void, it often interrupts the flow of anointing. Many churches hesitate to make adjustments because they are afraid of offending others. It is important to remain flexible if our churches are to flow in gifts and power.

A Spirit led Christian, and a body of believers that are led by the Holy Spirit seek God for direction, revelation and understanding before taking action. The Holy Spirit becomes the leader, as He should. Christians that are led by the Holy Spirit are open to exploring new ideas and place their confidence in knowing that they are following the directives of the Spirit, and therefore can expect positive results. When the Holy Spirit is consulted, He will help the right people find their place of anointed service so that the gifts flow with power and yield greater results.

Security in Financial Planning vs. Security in Kingdom Plans

Security and financial planning are important aspects of life that many people focus on in order to feel safe and secure. However, as Christians, our hope and trust should ultimately be anchored in God rather than in our financial situation. The Bible reminds us in Proverbs 3:5-6, "Trust in the Lord with all your heart and lean not on your own understanding; in all your ways submit to him, and he will make your paths straight." This means that we should trust God to provide for our needs, both financially and in all other areas of life. We can't predict the future. Many people have lost their financial security and find themselves badly shaken. That is understandable, but at the same time, it also reveals when a person has put their trust in the wrong thing. We must be careful that wealth does not become an idol. While it is important to be responsible with our finances and plan for the future, our ultimate security comes from God.

In the Kingdom of God, security is not based on earthly possessions or financial stability, but rather on our relationship with God. In Matthew 6:19-21, Jesus warns against storing up treasures on earth and encourages us to focus on storing up treasures in heaven. He goes on to say, "For where your treasure is, there your heart will be also." Our security in the Kingdom of God comes from our relationship with Him and our obedience to His will. As we seek first His kingdom and righteousness, He promises to provide for our needs (Matthew 6:33). While security and financial planning are important, as Christians our ultimate hope and trust should be anchored in God. We can find security in Him by trusting in His provision and storing up treasures in heaven. As we seek first His kingdom and righteousness, He promises to provide for us and guide us on the path He has for us.

Dutiful vs. Passionate

A dutiful person following God out of a sense of obligation recognizes the importance of fulfilling their duties and responsibilities as a believer. They may not always feel an emotional connection to God or experience a strong personal relationship with Him, but they believe that it is their obligation to live in accordance with the teachings of their faith. They may attend religious services, pray, and engage in acts of charity and service not necessarily out of personal desire, but because they feel it is their duty to do so. This may also result in a lack of good fruit in their life, because even though they attend church regularly, they may not allow God to actually change their heart and work on the deeper issues of their life. While their faith may not always feel easy or joyful, they recognize the value in fulfilling their obligations as a believer and seek to do so with sincerity and dedication.

On the other hand, a Christian who is passionate for God is someone who has a deep, burning desire to know God more intimately and to serve Him with their whole heart. They may spend long hours in prayer and study of the Bible, seeking to understand God's will for their life. Their passion for God is contagious, and they may inspire others to seek a deeper relationship with God as well. They embody the teachings of Christ in their actions and words. They are kind, patient, and loving towards others, and strive to live a life that reflects their faith. A passionate Christian displays the beauty of the Lord as they live out their faith in a way that inspires others and brings glory to God.

Faithful vs. Full of Faith

Being a faithful person implies a commitment to a set of beliefs or principles and a consistent adherence to them. A person can demonstrate faithfulness to their marriage vows and still live in a loveless, dead marriage. A person can show up to every church meeting and yet live in hypocrisy without allowing God to change their heart. Longevity is not always the mark of being faithful. A faithful person may be seen as someone who lives their life according to a particular faith or religion, but it can also refer to someone who is dedicated to a specific cause or belief system. People of other religions can be extremely committed, even to the point of sacrificing their life unto death, while their beliefs and actions have nothing to do with faith in Jesus Christ. Being faithful is not the evidence of living a life that pleases the Lord.

A person who has confident faith in Jesus Christ is someone who has faced the challenges and difficulties of life with the assurance that God is faithful and will never abandon them. They have weathered the storms of life and emerged stronger, more resilient, and more deeply rooted in their faith. Through their experiences, they have come to know Jesus Christ as a faithful and trustworthy friend who sustains them in times of trial and provides hope and peace that transcends all understanding. Their faith has been tested, refined, and strengthened, and they have learned to rely on God's grace and mercy to carry them through even the darkest moments of life. They are full of faith, like Caleb and Joshua, who had a confident expectation in God because they knew Him on a very personal level.

Plays it Safe vs. Takes Risks

Someone who always plays it safe may prefer to avoid taking risks or making bold moves, especially when it comes to their Christian faith. They may prioritize stability and security over stepping out in faith. For example, they may be hesitant to share their faith with others for fear of rejection or discomfort. When people put a higher priority on their comfort rather than on extending their faith, that timidity can cause them to stay stunted in their growth because they are reluctant to trust God in those situations. Hebrews 10:38 says: "...but the person who is righteous will live his life by trusting, and if he shrinks back, I will not be pleased with him." In Matthew 25:24-25, the servant who buried his talent instead of investing it was rebuked by his master. This parable highlights the importance of taking risks and using our gifts and resources wisely rather than playing it safe out of fear.

On the other hand, someone who takes risks for the sake of their Christian faith may be more willing to step out of their comfort zone and trust in God's plan for their life. They may take bold actions, such as leaving a stable job to pursue missionary work or standing up for their beliefs in the face of opposition. Leaving the ministry was a bold step, but I knew I needed to trust God for my future. I didn't know at the time how things were going to work out. Sowing my livelihood years later was also an extreme step, and it was rough, but we never would have seen the incredible miracles if we had not walked it out with God. When He sent us back to California, we had only enough to make it one way. We had no job, no connections to a place to live - nothing. All our belongings, a cat and our two very young children were packed up in our van. We put ourselves out on a limb and God began to move with divine connections. He worked through people we didn't even know and began to put the pieces together. He told us to go on a prayer walk. We did, and it led us to new relationships. It was His favor that opened new doors for a place to live and work. I have taken many risky steps of faith. Some worked out better than others, but God has never let me down. He loves it when we take a risk for the sake of faith. It pulls Him closer so that we can see Him move supernaturally. In Hebrews 11:6, it says "And without faith it is impossible to please God, because anyone who comes to him must believe that He exists and that He rewards those who earnestly seek Him."

Job vs. Calling

There are several differences between someone who is just working a job and someone who is working towards their calling in life. I have worked many odd jobs in my life, but they were simply a means to earning a paycheck. We all need to support ourselves and our families, and there is no shame in working the jobs that we have to, but many people do not always find a sense of fulfillment or purpose in just working at a job. There are also people who are willing to work hard and make sacrifices to achieve their goals without any clear sense of gratification as to why they are doing what they do. They are chasing money, bonuses, or the opportunity for a raise or promotion but their heart really isn't in the work itself.

On the other hand, someone who is working towards their calling in life has a clear sense of purpose and passion for what they do. They are driven by a deep sense of meaning and fulfillment that goes beyond just earning a paycheck. People who are working towards their calling tend to be motivated by the work itself rather than external rewards like money or status. Jesus said, "My food is to do the will of Him that sent me," and finish His work, (John 4:34). Jesus emphasized that fulfilling the purposes of God for His life was essential just like food was essential to his physical needs, and that it was the most important thing to Him. There are many things people can do with their life but most people do not get a sense of fulfillment unless they find a sense of purpose in what they're doing.

When people are working towards their calling, they are often more creative and innovative in their approach to their work. They are constantly looking for new and better ways to do things, and they are not afraid to take risks to achieve their goals. Those who are working towards their calling tend to take a long-term view of their careers. They are willing to invest time and effort into developing their skills and building their careers over the long term, even if it means taking on challenges and setbacks along the way. People who are working towards their calling are often focused on personal growth and development. They are committed to learning and growing as individuals, both personally and professionally. Overall, working towards a calling in life is often about finding meaning and fulfillment in one's work, while working a job is often more focused on earning a paycheck and meeting basic needs.

Service Minded vs. Gifts Minded

Being service-minded and gift-minded are both important aspects of living a faithful life, but they refer to different ways of expressing one's faith and serving others. It means having a heart for serving others and looking for opportunities to use one's skills and resources to help those in need. This can manifest in various ways, such as volunteering at a charity, donating to a cause, or simply offering a helping hand to a neighbor. All of those things are wonderful acts of service, but it does not require the assistance of the Holy Spirit and it may not be serving in the area of your gifting and calling. As Jesus said in Matthew 25:40, "Truly I tell you, whatever you did for one of the least of these brothers and sisters of mine, you did for me."

On the other hand, being gift-minded refers to having a spiritual gift or talent and using it to glorify God and edify others. This can include gifts such as teaching, preaching, encouragement, or music. These are spiritual gifts that come from the Holy Spirit, and are dependent upon Him as gifts to equip, teach, train and minister by the anointing to others. As the apostle Paul wrote in Romans 12:6-8, "We have different gifts, according to the grace given to each of us. If your gift is prophesying, then prophesy in accordance with your faith; if it is serving, then serve; if it is teaching, then teach; if it is to encourage, then give encouragement; if it is giving, then give generously; if it is to lead, do it diligently; if it is to show mercy, do it cheerfully."

It's important to remember that both service and spiritual gifts are given by God for the purpose of building up the body of Christ and advancing His kingdom. As 1 Peter 4:10-11 says, "Each of you should use whatever gift you have received to serve others, as faithful stewards of God's grace in its various forms. If anyone speaks, they should do so as one who speaks the very words of God. If anyone serves, they should do so with the strength God provides, so that in all things God may be praised through Jesus Christ. To him be the glory and the power for ever and ever. Amen."

Tither vs. Giver

The subject of tithing can divide people into two schools of thought: those that feel tithing is strictly an Old Testament principle, and those that feel it is still important today. Unfortunately, the subject of taking offerings can sometimes rub people the wrong way because it is often misused to apply pressure towards giving, which results in resentment in others. They may use passages such as Malachi 3:10, which speakers of bringing the whole tithe into the storehouse, to pressure people into giving more money. Sometimes those giving an offering message even declare that people are under a curse if they do not comply. However, this passage is actually directed towards the nation of Israel under the Old Covenant, not specifically towards modern day Christians. Some churches and leaders may focus more on the obligation to tithe rather than the heart behind it. This can create a sense of guilt or fear in individuals who may feel pressured to give, rather than inspired to give freely and joyfully.

Biblical tithing refers to the practice of giving 10% of one's income to support God's work. This practice is rooted in the Old Testament, where tithing was required of the Israelites as a way of supporting the Levites (Numbers 18:21-24) and the temple (Deuteronomy 12:5-6). They were instructed to give a tenth of their crops and livestock each year (Leviticus 27:30-32). Additionally, they were required to give other offerings and sacrifices throughout the year (Deuteronomy 16:16-17).

In the New Testament, Jesus affirmed the importance of tithing (Matthew 23:23) but also emphasized the importance of giving from the heart (Luke 21:1-4). In comparison, some churches today may take an offering every week or during every service, which can create a sense of pressure to give. However, it is important to remember that giving should be a personal decision made out of a joyful heart and a desire to support God's work.

Additionally, some churches may use the promise of prosperity or blessings as an incentive to give. While there are certainly blessings that come from giving, this should not be the primary motivation for generosity. God looks at our motivation, and it should be motivated by a desire to obey God and bless others.

When it comes to deciding what and how much to give, it is important to listen to the Holy Spirit and seek guidance from God. In 2 Corinthians 9:7, Paul writes, "Each of you should give what you have decided in your heart to give, not reluctantly or under compulsion, for God loves a cheerful giver." This means that we should pray about our giving and give what we feel led to give, rather than feeling pressured or obligated to give a certain amount.

Learning to listen to the Holy Spirit can be a process of developing our spiritual sensitivity and discernment. We can pray for guidance and ask the Holy Spirit to reveal to us what and how much to give. As we cultivate a closer relationship with God and seek to align our hearts with His will, we can become more attuned to His leading in all areas of our lives, including our giving. Ultimately, giving should be a joyful act of worship and obedience to God, rather than a source of guilt or pressure.

Man Pleaser vs. God Pleaser

A "man pleaser" is someone who prioritizes pleasing other people, often at the expense of their own values and beliefs. This can manifest as a desire to fit in, gain approval, or avoid conflict. Being a man pleaser can be considered an act of insincerity because it involves prioritizing the opinions and desires of others over one's own beliefs and values. In other words, a man pleaser may not be expressing their true thoughts and feelings, but instead going along with what they believe others want to hear or see. This lack of sincerity can lead to a lack of authenticity and trust in relationships.

Furthermore, being a man pleaser can be seen as a form of idolatry because it involves putting the opinions and desires of others above God. In the Bible, idolatry is defined as the worship of anything other than God, and this can include the worship of people's opinions, desires, or approval. One thing I've learned is that people's opinions change at whim. One moment they love you, the next moment you can't do anything right in their eyes. If you are living to please the opinions of others, you will never be happy because you've made others your gods. In Galatians 1:10, Apostle Paul warns against seeking the approval of man over God, saying that to do so would make one "not a servant of Christ." The Bible offers several examples of the dangers of being a man pleaser. In Galatians 1:10, Paul writes: "For am I now seeking the approval of man, or of God? Or am I trying to please man? If I were still trying to please man, I would not be a servant of Christ." Paul is emphasizing that seeking the approval of others can lead one away from God's plan and purpose.

Compromising one's integrity is another danger of being a man pleaser. When someone prioritizes pleasing others over their own values and beliefs, they may be tempted to compromise their integrity in order to fit in or gain approval. This can involve lying, cheating, or engaging in other unethical behavior in order to please others. Over time, compromising one's integrity can lead to a loss of self-respect and a lack of trust from others.

Finally, being a man pleaser can take a person into a form of bondage because it can create a cycle of constantly seeking the approval of others. When someone becomes dependent on the opinions and validation of others, they may feel trapped in a cycle of constantly trying to please others, even at the expense of their own well-being. This can create a sense of bondage and powerlessness, as the person feels unable to break free from the need for approval.

In contrast, someone who wants to please God will prioritize obedience to God's commands over pleasing others. An example of this is the Apostle Peter, who in Acts 4:19-20 tells the religious leaders who are threatening him and John: "Whether it is right in the sight of God to listen to you rather than to God, you must judge, for we cannot but speak of what we have seen and heard." Peter is making it clear that he will not compromise his obedience to God in order to please human authorities.

In summary, a man pleaser prioritizes pleasing others, while someone who wants to please God prioritizes loyalty and obedience to God's commands. The Bible offers numerous examples of the dangers of being a man pleaser, and the importance of prioritizing obedience to God over pleasing others.

Restricted Vision vs. Global Vision

A Christian with a restricted vision is someone that prioritizes the needs and interests of their local church community over the needs of the larger Christian community. They may be resistant to change or new ideas. and seem inflexible to doing things differently. They are more of an "in the box" type of personality and prefer a set way of doing things.They may serve their local church but not be concerned with the Christian community in other locations.

Many pastors and leaders are so consumed by the commitments to their own church and ministries that it becomes very difficult to schedule any outside activities with other organizations. An overloaded schedule is understandable, but it can result in a restricted vision.

A person with a global vision, however, is more likely to look for creative solutions outside the box. They are focused on sharing the gospel with as many people as possible, regardless of their background or location. They may be involved in mission work or other forms of outreach as they explore new ideas and opportunities to enlarge the influence of the Kingdom of God.

Diplomatic vs. Warrior

A diplomatic person is someone that is polite and careful not to offend others. They are very sensitive to how certain things may come across to others and try to be tactful in how they respond to people. The challenge with this is because people that are trying to make everyone happy often compromise in order to keep the peace. They fail to see spiritual warfare tactics at work. The enemy looks for opportunities to neutralize the power and effectiveness of the Holy Spirit, and Satan is willing to take advantage where he can slowly, bit by bit, one little compromise at a time. Pastors deal with many people that want to influence their decisions. If their goal is to keep the peace, they will be open to compromise on spiritual matters, thinking it won't do any harm. Satan is very patient in his assignment to bind the church, therefore we must be warriors in the Spirit, praying, seeking God's wisdom, and not allowing the complaints or pressure from others lead us into making peace treaties with the enemy.

A warrior, on the other hand, is someone that is led by the Holy Spirit and doesn't allow the opinions of others to lead them away from the wisdom of God and direction that He has shown them. When praying for wisdom, ask the Holy Spirit to give you the Spirit of Understanding as to the true motives of others. It may take some time for those things to be revealed, so don't be in a rush to make a decision on something you're unclear about. People often have their own reasons for doing things, but you need to discern whether or not their motives are pure, and if they are speaking by the influence of the Holy Spirit or a different spirit. Sometimes wisdom looks like taking a stand rather than giving in to the demands of others. Even polite words that sound like wisdom may not be in line with the will of God. Remember that the enemy is always looking for opportunities to have us concede in pressure situations because if we do, we surrender our power and authority. Sometimes it is better to walk away rather than allow the desire for peace to trick you into making a compromise that is unwise.

Needs Recognition vs. Gives Recognition

An emotionally immature and needy person who needs motivation typically relies on others to provide them with the emotional support and encouragement that they need to take action or make decisions. They may struggle with self-confidence or have difficulty setting and achieving goals on their own. They may also be overly dependent on others for validation or approval, and may become anxious or upset when they do not receive the attention or recognition they feel they deserve.

On the other hand, a person who motivates others is someone who inspires and encourages others to take action or pursue their goals. They may have a natural ability to inspire and lead others, and may be skilled at identifying and nurturing the strengths and talents of those around them. They may be driven by a passion or sense of purpose, and may be able to communicate their vision and ideas in a way that inspires others to get behind them.

While there may be some overlap in these two types of individuals, the key difference is that someone who is emotionally immature and needy is focused on receiving support and validation from others, while someone who motivates others is focused on empowering and helping others to achieve their goals.

Appointed by Man vs. Appointed by God

There are many things to consider when it comes to choosing leaders. God's choice often looks completely different than man's ideal candidate. A leadership selection process also goes through a human process which is often influenced by a number of factors. Academic achievements, public speaking skills, a charismatic personality and people's personal opinions and relationship to various candidates are given weight to the decision making process. However, none of those things reveal a person's character or integrity, which are tested by God. Man's selection process is unable to determine an individual's commitment level to God, or whether or not they have paid the price to qualify for the position they seek. For example, King Saul looked like a worthy candidate for leadership and was chosen by the people of Israel to be their king, but he had many character weaknesses that caused him to disobey God and be rejected as His appointed leader, (1 Samuel 15). God began looking for King Saul's replacement successor many years before Saul was disqualified, so that when the time was right, His man was adequately prepared and trained by the Holy Spirit to be ready to lead God's people.

God selected a young shepherd boy named David, who by all outward appearances might seem to be unfit for the role as a future King. Not only was David the youngest of his brothers, they despised him. 1 Samuel 16:7 tells an important truth. God does not evaluate people for leadership according to the same standards as man's selection process. David's father, Jesse, as well as his brothers thought Eliab, one of David's brothers, would be anointed as the next king, but Samuel said, 'The Lord said to Samuel, "Do not look at his appearance or his physical stature, because I have refused him. For the Lord does not see as man sees; for man looks at the outward appearance, but the Lord looks at the heart." One by one, David's brothers were rejected from being called as the next king. But, God would not allow David to be overlooked in His selection process. The prophet Samuel had David called in from the field where he was tending the sheep and anointed him with oil. (1 Samuel 16:13). As an adult, David had some serious missteps and mistakes, yet they did not disqualify him from his kingly role. God's leaders are selected despite their weaknesses, but according to His divine will, and they are empowered to carry out His exploits.

These are just some of the differences between the church and the kingdom. God's glory is to spread like a river that proceeds from the throne of God, flowing through faith-filled hearts. God's glory will not flow through an unbelieving people that are marked by pride, self-will and selfish ambition. Many people have constructed walls of pride, self-preservation, and offense. They protect their wounds with unforgiveness, criticism, and condemnation. There are other walls of legalism and religious differences. Some of these walls are made up of jealousy, prejudice, racism, competition and distrust. These are walls that separate us and cause disunity to remain between us. The walls can only come down through transparency and overcoming our fears of what others might think about us. Transparency is what allows a healing process to take place in ourselves and others that hear our stories. We lose power and effectiveness when we remain disconnected from one another. It hurts God's heart to see His family so disconnected with one another. When Jesus prayed in John 17:20-24, He said: "I do not pray for these alone, but also for those who will believe in Me through their word; that they may all be one just as we are one. I in them, and You in Me; that they may be made perfect in one and that the world may know that You have sent Me, and have loved them and You have loved Me." Jesus went on to say in verse 24: "...that they may behold My glory." God's glory is revealed every time we defeat the giants that stand in opposition to our faith. Giants of fear and intimidation mock our faith and our God as they tell us we will look like fools if we allow ourselves to be transparent with our stories of failure, sin and shame. Yet, it's our stories of these very things that become the well-placed stones that take down the giants, because the story never ends with what we've done to make a mess of things. The story becomes a testimony of hope to others as we let down our guard and tell how our amazing God met us at our lowest and pulled us out of a pit, or how the God of the impossible met us in our impossible circumstances and saved the day. That is what people love to hear because it bears witness to a supernatural God that loves us enough to get involved in our lives. It's those soul-baring, risk taking occasions when we share our testimonies that become a lifeline of hope and healing to others, and they are anointed for breakthrough. Conquering our fears also strips the enemy of his ability to keep us locked up behind walls of fear and self-preservation. God is looking for humble people that put their trust in Him so that He can move in love, power, forgiveness and release restoration. Fires of revival will burn more and more as people operate in humility and love. The walls will come down to enable us as a body to embrace honesty instead of pride, and love instead of hypocrisy. The fire of God's glory will spread throughout the land as hearts are revived.

The Kingdom of God needs men and women who will boldly preach the Word of God, break bondages and set the captives free. We must declare that we are taking ground away from the enemy. We are a storehouse for the world in a time of famine. God is placing a hunger in people for the Bread of Life - *Jesus*. The pain and oppression of captivity drives people to cry out for freedom. The United States prides itself on independence yet, sadly we are one of the most imprisoned people on earth. The demands to live as we please are really a false sense of freedom and a deception. Addictions, lust, greed, selfishness and idolatry can be some of the hardest taskmasters. True freedom comes from unburdening our soul through confession, repentance, and obeying God's commands. His forgiveness and mercy flows to us as we forgive others. God is preparing His servants to open those storehouse doors of ministry to desperate people. There are generations of people yearning for what is genuinely the ministry of Jesus. Our God is an awesome God and He is sovereign in the earth today. He visits His field and waters it. He provides rich abundance for the continuance of the ministry He has ordained and established. In the Book of Revelation, Jesus is seen walking amid the churches with His lampstand, looking at the branches and pruning those that bear no fruit. The Holy Spirit came to bring a seal on every fruit that is harvested and exported. The seal testifies, "This fruit is Son kissed, produced in the garden of the Father.

CONCLUSION

Whether or not you are planted in a constricted environment or in a spacious place where you can reach your full potential is key to whether or not your job, career or ministry will become a blessing that will fulfill God's dream for your life. I am a man that had to have my pot broken and leave my comfort zone in order to receive the kingdom. If you find yourself in that place, do not fear. Transition is an uncomfortable place because it is a constant state of change. It is also a place of death and resurrection. Death to the old way of living, death to ourselves, death to needing to have all the answers, and surrendering our rights to feel hurt, disappointed, and offended because God no longer works according to how we think He should act. We have to surrender all of it, simply trusting that God loves us and He knows what He's doing. We learn to listen to His voice, and not rush to make decisions based only on what we see, because He is often busy doing something on our behalf that hasn't been revealed. He leads us even when we feel we're in the dark. Sometimes the purpose isn't understood until later, and we just have to be okay with that. Peace comes through surrender and trust. Transition is full of trials. tests, and pressure situations that force what's in us to rise to the surface so that we can acknowledge character deficits, works of the flesh, wrong beliefs and areas where our soul needs healing.

God has promised to never leave us or forsake us. His grace will see us through anything we face. Transition is a time when we learn how to trust God more and more, as we forget the things that are behind us and look forward with confidence to what lies ahead of us. We learn new strategies such as humility, love, vulnerability and transparency, for these are the things that utterly defeat the enemy. And, when it seems as if the season will never change, remember not to throw away your confidence. Though the promise tarries, wait for it. It will surely come at the appointed time. Be strong and courageous and wait patiently for the Lord. There will come a day when everything that is false will be separated from what is genuine. Let us not trade the pearl of great price for things that lack true wealth and lasting riches with eternal value. Our destiny has been set and our future is bright. Let us go on with confidence and boldly pray, "Lord, Your kingdom come. Your will be done. On earth, as it is in heaven."

ROOM TO GROW

ABOUT THE AUTHOR

Norm Gagnon is a revivalist minister that loves to encourage others through kingdom teaching and ministers in prophetic worship ministry, teaching and deliverance. He shares powerful teaching and insights that expose the darkness, reveal the heart of God, and equip the believer to live a victorious life in Christ. His desire is for every believer to experience freedom, healing and personal revival, and to see cities transformed by the power and presence of God. The Gagnons are married and live in Lake Elsinore, California. You may contact Norm at: xpectamiracle@yahoo.com. Please visit: www.xpectamiracleministries.com and www.lakeelsinoreoutpouring.com for more information.

Made in the USA
Coppell, TX
23 May 2023

17198962R00066